Effective Client Interviewing and Counseling

O.J. Salinas
Clinical Associate Professor of Law
University of North Carolina Law School

A SHORT & HAPPY GUIDE® SERIES

WEST
ACADEMIC
PUBLISHING

444 Cedar Street, Suite 700
St. Paul, MN 55101
1-877-888-1330

Printed in the United States of America

ISBN: 978-1-63460-408-6

Preface

Law students may sometimes forget that many people, companies, and organizations are directly impacted by the work that lawyers do. I know that I may have forgotten this at times when I was a student. I was often too worried about getting called on in class to truly appreciate that the critical lawyerly thinking that was taking place in my Socratic classes was going to help me provide good, sound legal advice to my clients.

It took me a while to understand and appreciate that our legal analysis, legal writing, and oral advocacy all relate to clients! Our clients will be facing some situation that prompts them to seek legal advice; they will be facing some "legal problem." But, we can't effectively provide this legal advice to our clients if we can't first have a conversation with our clients.

This book provides an introduction to how we might have a conversation with our clients. The book begins with a discussion about the need for more skills-based courses in law school—like interviewing and counseling. Parts 2 and 3 of the book discuss and demonstrate how attorneys can effectively communicate with clients in a client interview. Part 4 of the book provides a basic outline for an initial client interview. Part 5 of the book highlights some basic counseling skills that attorneys can use to more effectively communicate with their clients.

Parts 3, 4, and 5 of the book include hypothetical exchanges between an attorney and a client. While most of the book and the exchanges focus on a conversation between an attorney and a client in an *initial client interview,* many of the skills and techniques discussed and demonstrated can be applied to client interviews that may occur throughout the course of our representation of our clients.

Since the majority of the book is focused on having a conversation with our clients, I have tried to write the book as if I am having a conversation with you. So, you will see that many of my sentences may start with the word "so." And, yes, you will see that many of my sentences may start with the words "and" or "yes." I may even throw in some commas, periods, or dashes in my sentences where they may not be grammatically needed. Think of these extra commas, periods, and dashes as the natural pauses that I might make during a conversation with you.

So, yes, I have tried to write this book as if I am having a conversation with you. And, by you, I mean a law student or legal professional. Whether you are a law student who has never worked with a client, or whether you are a seasoned attorney looking for a refresher on the basics to effective client interviewing and counseling, *you* can use this book. I hope you enjoy *A Short and Happy Guide to Effective Client Interviewing and Counseling*.[1]

O.J. Salinas

January 2016

---

[1] One more thing—I know some of you reading this book are still law students. But, throughout the book, I might often refer to "you" as attorneys or licensed attorneys. You are in law school. You are learning to think like lawyers. You work with clients, or you will soon be working with clients. So, even though you may not have your law license yet, I am assuming that you are part of the profession. And, throughout the book, I will ask that you, too, try to become an effective attorney *and* counselor!

Acknowledgments

I am thankful that Paula Franzese had the vision to start the *Short and Happy Guide* series. I used law school supplements when I was a student. I use law school supplements in my working with my law students. I think the *Short and Happy Guide* series is a great resource for law students, and I am thankful to be able to join the series.

To Doris: You encouraged me to pursue my Master's in Counseling after years of seeing me work as a litigator. You saw that I could combine my interest in conflict resolution and counseling skills with my work in law. Thank you for being my rock, my friend, and my partner. Thank you also for your great feedback on the book. It was such a benefit to be able to bounce ideas off a psychiatrist!

To Jordan and Evan: You make me laugh. You show me unconditional love. You are wonderful children, and I am grateful that I am your father.

To the rest of my family and friends: Thank you so much for your love and support. I would also like to express special thanks to my colleagues, Kaci Bishop and Alexa Chew, for their sound feedback on the book.

Table of Contents

A Short & Happy Guide to Effective Client Interviewing and Counseling

PART 1

Attorneys *and* Counselors—We Are Both, Folks!

CHAPTER 1

A Law License
Wake-Up Call

When I look up at my law license, I see a nicely framed certificate that I paid too much for. The certificate "certifies" three things:

1. That I "fulfilled all of the requirements of law;"

2. That I "subscribed to the official oath" of office for newly licensed attorneys; and

3. That, "upon the motion of the Board of Law Examiners," I am "duly admitted and licensed as an "ATTORNEY _AND_ COUNSELOR AT LAW."[1]

It has been over fifteen years since I joined the ranks of licensed attorneys (yes, I am getting old). When I graduated law school, I knew that I was going to work as an attorney. When I passed the dreaded bar examination and took my oath of office, I knew that I was a "licensed attorney." But, I really didn't think of

---

[1] Okay. So, I am adding emphasis here. My law license does capitalize the phrase "attorney and counselor at law." But, unfortunately, the license doesn't underline or italicize the phrase. It would really help the premise of my book if it did!

myself as an "attorney _and_ counselor." I would venture to say that many law students and licensed attorneys feel the same way. After all, how many of us answer, "I am an attorney _and_ counselor" when we are asked what we do for a living? Or, did any of us ever say, "I want to be an attorney _and_ counselor when I grow up?"

But, my law license "certifies" that I am an attorney and counselor. So, I guess I am both. Or, at least, I have been both since 1999 (a great _Prince_ song, by the way!).

CHAPTER 2

Law School Curriculum—Changes Are Coming

A. The Basic Law School Curriculum: Doctrine over Skills?

So, my law license says that I am an attorney and counselor. And your law license should, too. Even if it doesn't, you will still be expected to "counsel" your clients on their legal matters. You will still be expected to have some so-called "soft skills"—like effective client interviewing and counseling.

But, many of us never take an interviewing and counseling class in law school. We take the required legal research and writing courses. We take the standard first-year doctrinal courses. We take many substantive courses that will be tested on our state bar exams. And we often take some upper-level writing seminars that examine some nuanced area of law that we will likely never use in practice.

We learn a lot about doctrine in law school, or at least we sit in classrooms where doctrine is discussed. But, we often forget that there is more to the practice of law than just the substantive law:

- Outside of the law school classroom, there will be clients.

- These clients will have legal problems.

- We will need to have conversations with our clients to learn the facts related to their problems.

- We will use what we learned in law school to find the relevant law and analyze how this law applies to our clients' problems.

- We will need to have conversations with our clients to advise them on how the law applies to their problems.

- Throughout the course of our representation of our clients, we will need to interview and counsel our clients.

So, my law license does not lie. Well, it sort of *lies* on the wall in my office. But, it does not lie when it reads that I am an attorney *and* counselor. Yes. Throughout the course of our representation of one client, we may have to interview and counsel the client several times. Sometimes when we interview and counsel clients, our focus will just be on understanding our clients' stories—the reasons why they are seeking an attorney, their problems, and the facts related to their problems *as they describe them to us*. Sometimes, we may be advising our clients on how the law applies to their problems. Sometimes, we may be seeking additional facts that might help us distinguish a particular legal authority or help prepare our cases for mediation. And sometimes, we may be counseling our clients on how to protect them from future litigation or how to move forward with a particular transaction.

There are many reasons why we interview and counsel a client. And there are many reasons why practical skills, like interviewing and counseling, should be better incorporated in the law school curriculum.

B. *Carnegie*, Employers, and Clients—Oh, My!

I'm not trying to be a bummer. But, the legal education that you embarked upon has been facing some significant criticism. One such criticism emerged in 2007, from *The Carnegie Foundation for the Advancement of Teaching* ("*The Carnegie Report*").[1]

The Carnegie Report concluded that the typical law school curriculum provides "relatively little attention to direct training in professional practice." It advised that law students "need a dynamic curriculum that moves them back and forth between understanding and enactment, [and] experience and analysis." At its foundation, the criticism from *The Carnegie Report* was quite simple: You are professional schools; teach your students how to work in the profession.

So, law schools have been feeling the pressure to make their law school graduates more "practice-ready." In addition to *The Carnegie Report*, legal employers have been frustrated that new law school graduates are not ready to effectively represent a client when they graduate from law school. Clients have also rightfully been refusing to pay *to train* their attorneys to practice law. After all, law school *is* a professional school. And most law

---

[1] William M. Sullivan, Anne Colby, Judith Welch Wegner, Lloyd Bond, & Lee S. Shulman, EDUCATING LAWYERS: PREPARATION FOR THE PROFESSION OF LAW (Jossey-Bass 2007). A summary of *The Carnegie Report* can be found at http://archive.carnegie foundation.org/pdfs/elibrary/elibrary_pdf_632.pdf.

school graduates enter the legal profession *to practice law*. So, it makes sense that law schools should want their graduates to be ready to practice law. It really does.

1. *Law School Curriculum: The Medical School Model*

As a result of the demands to train law school students to be more practice-ready, law schools have examined the curriculum from other professional schools—such as medical schools.

Medical schools require students to start working with patients early on in their medical school education. For example, in addition to learning pharmacology and where the adrenal glands are located in the human body, medical students get trained *to practice medicine*. What a concept! Students not only have to use their knowledge of medicine and science to diagnose a particular patient's complaint early on in their medical school education, but they have to interact with the patient to help counsel the patient on his diagnosis.

Medical schools have been training their medical students on "soft skills"—like interviewing and counseling—for many, many years. This direct training in the professional practice of medicine helps combine the science and doctrine of medicine with the practical skills that physicians use on a daily basis in their profession. But, how many law schools can truly say that they have been directly and effectively training the majority of their graduates to practice law?

2. Law School Curriculum: More Practice-Ready Courses

Law schools have traditionally offered clinics and externships to help expose their students to the practice of law. Additionally, law schools might offer courses in negotiation, interviewing, and client-counseling to help teach students the art of working with and advising clients on their legal matters. However, these experiential and simulation courses are often taught in smaller-sized sections, and they may only be offered every other semester. Logistically, the size and frequency of the courses limit the number of students who can benefit from the training.

As a result of the frustration from legal employers that many law school graduates are not ready to practice law and the refusal from clients to pay to help train lawyers, the American Bar Association (ABA) has now required law schools to provide more "experiential" courses—where students can combine legal doctrine with practical lawyering skills. Law schools can satisfy the experiential coursework requirements through traditional course offerings, like clinics and field placement work. Law schools can also satisfy the experiential coursework requirements through "simulation" courses—courses that are "reasonably similar to the experience of a lawyer advising or representing a client or engaging in other lawyering tasks in a set of facts and circumstances devised or adopted by a faculty member."[2] In other words, law schools may be able to satisfy the new ABA requirement for more experiential courses in classes where students are provided with hypothetical case files. With these

---

[2] The American Bar Association's *Standards and Rules of Procedure for Approval of Law Schools* can be found at http://www.americanbar.org/groups/ legal_education/resources/standards.html. The standards for experiential and simulation courses can be found in Chapter 3, Program of Legal Education.

hypothetical case files, students can engage in "lawyering tasks," such as drafting court documents, working with affidavits and depositions, and—of course!—interviewing and counseling a client.

Parts 3-5 of the book provide several demonstrations of hypothetical exchanges between an attorney and client. I use the hypothetical exchanges to help demonstrate the problem-solving aspect of our jobs as attorneys *and* counselors. Whether you are doing simulated client interviews in a law school class, or whether you are getting ready to work with a client in your law office conference room, you can use the hypothetical exchanges as practice and guidance on how to conduct an effective client interview. You can use this book to help strengthen your ability to become an effective attorney *and* counselor.

CHAPTER 3

Problem-Solving Attorneys and Counselors

A. The Legal Profession and Math Class?

How many of you remember word problems from your math classes? Remember reading those paragraph-like stories about Max having eight times as many baseball cards as Serena? If Serena has seven baseball cards, how many cards does Max have?

Some of you may be cringing right now from bad memories of algebra or multiplication tables. But, those word problems may have helped you prepare to be effective client counselors. To help you work through your grade school word problems and solve for the missing variable, you likely were instructed to ask yourself a few questions:

- What is the question that I am being asked to answer?

- What information do I have available to help me answer the question?

Now, think about a word problem in terms of an attorney-client interview. Let's assume you don't know much about the client's problem before the client walks inside the conference room for the client interview. In other words, there is no paragraph-like story in front of you that gives you the information you need to help answer the question. Instead, you have to talk to the client to get this information. In doing so, you can ask yourself the same type of questions you were instructed to ask yourself back in your grade school days—plus one more:

- What is the question that I am being asked to answer?

- What information do I have available to help me answer the question?

- What information do I need to get from the client to help me answer the question?

Now let's turn back to the Max and Serena baseball card word problem. For this example, let's assume that Max has no mathematical skills. Let's also assume that the reason he is seeking assistance is to find an answer to the word problem. An initial client interview with Max could look like this:

* * *

Attorney:	Hello, Max.
Client:	Hi.
Attorney:	Thanks for coming into the office. How may I help you today?
Client:	Well, I got a bunch of baseball cards. And I'd like to find out how many I have.

Attorney:	Okay. So, it sounds like you are interested in just finding out how many baseball cards you have.
Client:	Yes.
Attorney:	Okay. Good. Well, before I can answer your question, I have a few questions myself. These questions will help me better assist you.
Client:	Okay. Go right ahead.
Attorney:	Great. So, did you happen to bring your baseball cards with you? I could help you count them.
Client:	Well, no. I didn't bring them with me.
Attorney:	Okay. Well, that may make things a little more difficult for us. I wonder if there is any other information that you can share with me that might be related to your baseball card collection question.
Client:	Let me see. Well, I remember that my sister said that I have eight times as many baseball cards as my friend, Serena.
Attorney:	Wonderful. So, you have eight times as many baseball cards as your friend, Serena. Would you happen to know how many cards Serena has?
Client:	Yes. She has seven baseball cards.
Attorney:	Great. That is really helpful information, Max.
Client:	Okay.

Attorney:	If you have eight times as many baseball cards as Serena, and Serena has seven baseball cards, then you should have a total of fifty-six baseball cards.
Client:	Great! Thanks so much.

* * *

The above example may seem simple. It contains some basic mathematical skills that many of us can perform through what I hear is called "mental-math." On the other hand, some of you may hate me for stirring up some mathematical-related anxiety. But, the point is that your prior experience with word problems can help you through an attorney-client interview:

- Your client will present with a problem.

- You will need some information from the client to help answer the problem.

- You will use the law by applying it to the facts of your client's problem.

- Based on this legal analysis, you will communicate an answer to your client or advise your client on how best to move forward with his problem.

B. A Different Type of Word Problem?

Many of us may have decided to go to law school because we did not like solving math problems. Well, folks, the truth is all of us in the legal profession are problem solvers. We are just solving a different type of problem. We still are trying to find the best possible answer to a client's problem. We still have to check and show our work. And, yes, occasionally, we still need to use some of our arithmetic skills.

If you are a practicing lawyer, you are helping others solve their legal problems. It doesn't matter if you are interested in civil, criminal, litigation, or transactional work. Legal professionals are problem solvers no matter what type of law they practice.

What about the size and location of your firm or non-profit? Same thing. You are helping solve problems no matter if you are working in one of the largest law firms in New York City or if you are a sole practitioner in a two-stoplight town.

We are problem solvers when we are defending a huge corporation in a multi-million dollar lawsuit. We are problem solvers when we are prosecuting a defendant in a state criminal proceeding. And we are problem solvers when we are protecting the rights of a spouse who wants to ensure that he gets the entire set of videotape recordings for the television show *Murder, She Wrote* in a divorce settlement. (Videotape recordings? *Murder, She Wrote*? Look them up, young folks! And while you are at it, consider taking a look at a certain music playing device known as a *Walkman*!).

CHAPTER 4

Multiple Hat-Wearing Problem Solvers

A. How Many Hats Can You Wear?

There are many aspects to our job as problem solvers. As such, we must wear many hats in our quest to be effective practicing attorneys. For example:

- We must be able to market ourselves in such a way that clients will be able to find us if and when they do have a problem;

- We must be able to have some understanding of the law in our jurisdiction, or at least know how to locate and update the law in our jurisdiction;

- We must also be able to apply this law to the facts of our particular client's case; and

- We must be able to communicate, verbally and in writing, this application of law to the facts of our client's case;

Seems like a lot of work already. But, our job as problem solvers doesn't stop there.

B. A Word Problem with No Words?

No. Our job as problem solvers doesn't stop there. We won't have anything to research about if we don't know what our client's problem is to begin with. We won't be able to apply whatever law is out there if we don't know the facts of our client's case. We won't be able to help solve our client's problem if we can't have a conversation with the client about how and why he needs our assistance. Similar to the Max baseball card interview example, we can't solve that word problem without some exchange of words with our client. We have to join the club and become effective attorney-client counselors. Fortunately, that's the title to Part 2 of the book!

Join the Club! You, Too, Can Be an Effective Attorney-Client Counselor

CHAPTER 5

Building a Bridge to a Strong Professional Relationship with Our Clients

Our success in helping our clients solve their problems often depends on how effective we are in developing strong professional relationships with them. Strong professional relationships don't require that we be friends with our clients. Certainly, you are not required or expected to have weekend barbecues with your clients. Nor, should you expect an invitation from your client for her son's high school graduation.

Strong professional relationships build on comfort and communication. Effective interviewing and client counseling skills can facilitate the development of a strong professional relationship with our clients. Effective interviewing and client counseling skills can help build trust and rapport.

A. Reminiscing—Good and Bad Conversations

Think back to those great conversations that you have had with another person (sorry, self-talk doesn't really help here). I am talking about those really fulfilling conversations where you felt like:

- The other person was really getting what you were saying; or

- You were really getting what the other person was saying.

What did you like about the conversation? What do you think you did to help make the conversation a strong one? What did the other person do? Did you already know this person well? If not, what happened that made you want to spend some time speaking with this person?

Now, think back to those conversations you have had with another person that you felt were just bad or unfulfilling. What did you dislike about the conversation? What do you think you did to help make the conversation a bad one? What did the other person do? Did you already know this person well? If not (and assuming that this conversation did not occur during a mugging or some other crime), what happened that made you want to get as far away from this person as soon as you could?

B. You Are on the Right Track, Already!

For those really great conversations, you probably felt like the other person was really listening to you. You likely received cues from the other person that made you believe that what you were saying mattered to this person. I imagine that there was good eye contact between the two of you. I imagine that you were not rolling your eyes or constantly yawning while the other person spoke. I imagine that the other person was not fixated on some new game on his smartphone during the conversation.

Perhaps, one or both of you paraphrased what the other person said. Perhaps, one or both of you acknowledged some of the values or emotions relating to the content of the conversation. Perhaps, one or both of you felt like the conversation had a beginning, middle, and end.

Many of the techniques that you consciously or subconsciously have used in creating strong conversations with other people are the same techniques that will make you an effective attorney *and* counselor. So, you are on the right track already! These techniques, and others, will be addressed further in Parts 3, 4, and 5 of this book.

CHAPTER 6

The Importance of Communication

A. You Don't Have to Be a Talker to Be an Effective Communicator

Many of us are not extroverted. I know I don't like to be the center of attention, and I prefer to slowly and quietly think about things before I speak. I remember feeling shocked at how freely and willingly students participated in the law school Socratic class, while I sat on my hands in the back of the classroom praying that I would not get called on.

Well, I got through law school and a litigation practice. And, now I teach in a law school. So, you can learn, practice, and teach law even if you were not a student who sat up in the front rows of class and *wanted* to be called on. I have learned that you don't have to be a talker to be an effective communicator—and you can, too.

B. I'd Prefer to Just Sit in My Office and Not Speak to Anyone

Sorry. You may not want to speak to anyone. But, practicing law requires you to speak to other people.

Yes. Quiet time is good. Meditation and self-reflection can rejuvenate you. And you will likely spend a lot of time *alone* in your office or in the library reading statutes, case law, and administrative regulations. But, the truth is no one practices law in a vacuum. At some point, attorneys need to speak with at least some other person. This person may be the opposing counsel. This person may be the judge. This person may be a mediator. And, yes, this person definitely may be the client.

Part of our job as problem solvers includes counseling our clients. And counseling our clients requires communication. We don't have to be the most eloquent speakers to effectively counsel our clients. We don't have to be the most confident public speakers, either. We just need to be able to have a conversation with our clients. And unless you have been on some deserted island for your entire life, you likely have had many conversations with many people prior to your first day of law school. Even if you have been on a deserted island, you may have had a conversation with one or two volleyballs. I hear that some folks can have quite the conversation with the *Wilson* brand of volleyballs. Just ask *Tom Hanks*.

C. The Five Pillars to the Conversation Foundation—An Introduction

So, you just need to have a conversation with the client. Yes. This conversation will involve some exchange of information relevant to a particular legal issue. But, communicating with your client doesn't have to be difficult. Consider the following bullet list as the five pillars for the foundation to a conversation with your client:

- **PILLAR 1:** Let the clients know you are there to help them.

- **PILLAR 2:** Let the clients talk.

- **PILLAR 3:** Listen.

- **PILLAR 4:** Try to understand the clients' stories.

- **PILLAR 5:** Take time to explain to the clients, in layman's terms, how the law applies to their problems.

These pillars often overlap with and build upon one another. In other words, they are not entirely separate steps to building a strong conversation with your clients. Much like a support system to the foundation of a house or building, the pillars work together to build a strong conversation foundation.

You will find more details and some examples of the pillars to the conversation foundation in Part 3 of the book. Further elaboration on the pillars is included within the outline to a client interview in Part 4 of the book.

Let's Work with the Conversation Foundation!

Communication is key when working with clients. We are not going to be able to maintain a steady stream of clients if our clients don't feel like they are respected and understood. Some of our communications with our clients will be in writing (shout out to all of you Legal Research and Writing Faculty!). Other communication will be done orally.

Our oral communication with our clients will likely influence how strong a professional relationship we build with them. Following the pillars to the conversation foundation introduced in Chapter 6 may help us become more effective oral communicators with our clients. Chapters 7-11 of the book describe each pillar. These chapters illustrate how each pillar to the conversation foundation could play out in an initial attorney-client interview for a hypothetical premises liability case.

For the premises liability case, I provide what I think are effective exchanges between the attorney and client. I cleverly call these exchanges "effective" conversations with the client. I also provide a few ineffective exchanges between the attorney and client. Yep! You guessed it! I refer to these exchanges as "ineffective" conversations.

As you read through Chapters 7-11, I hope you get a feel for the techniques that the attorney is using to develop trust and rapport with the client during the initial client interview. I also hope you begin to recognize how the pillars of the conversation foundation can work together to make you a more effective attorney *and* counselor.

Let's dive in and work with the conversation foundation!

CHAPTER 7

The First Pillar—Let the Clients Know You Are There to Help Them

The first pillar to the conversation foundation is to let the clients know that you are there to help them. Let's examine it further.

A. I Am Your Attorney. Please Don't Fear or Hate Me.

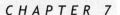

Many clients have never worked with an attorney before. Their only experience with attorneys may be watching hotheaded litigators fighting on television. These clients may not know that attorneys can be compassionate. These clients may not know that attorneys can be good listeners. These clients may not understand that attorneys are there to help them.

On the other hand, we may represent a client who had a bad experience with a prior attorney. Perhaps, this client felt like the attorney never reported back to her what was happening with her lawsuit. Perhaps, during the initial interview, the client felt like the attorney was just "going through the motions" to bill his hourly rate. Perhaps, the client felt like the attorney didn't really care about her.

When our clients don't really feel like we are there to help them, they may be less inclined to give us the information we need to best serve them. They may withhold significant facts. They may forget to tell us something because they feel like we are disinterested. They may be nervous or confused. They may not trust us.

One way to start building trust is to establish rapport. We can start building this important bond with our clients by simply saying that we are there to help them. But when we are expressing our desire to help our clients, we should strive to be believable. I am not saying that we need to be an *Oscar*-winning actor to pull this off, but we need to seem honest and sincere. We should be cognizant that the tone of our voice can impact how our clients view us. We should also try to acknowledge any initial thoughts, concerns, or expectations that the clients may have that relate to their legal problems. Consider the following example:

* * *

Attorney:	Hello, Ms. James. Thank you so much for coming by the office this morning. This is my paralegal, Stacy Garcia. I know you have spent some time speaking with Stacy over the telephone. She will be sitting in on the interview with me today and will help take notes of what is said during the interview.
Client:	Yes. Hello, Stacy.
Paralegal:	Hello, Ms. James.

Attorney:	So, Ms. James. Did you have any trouble finding our office?
Client:	Oh, no. It was easy.
Attorney:	Good. Well, Ms. James, we understand that you have received a letter that states that you are going to be sued in state court.
Client:	Yes. I received the letter a few days ago, and I have been worrying about it ever since. I have never been sued. I don't know what to do.
Attorney:	We understand that this must be very difficult for you, Ms. James. Receiving a letter that threatens a lawsuit against you can be very upsetting—especially if you have never been sued before.
Client:	Yes. It is very upsetting.
Attorney:	Well, the good thing is that you are here today and that you are seeking legal representation. We have handled similar lawsuits before. And we are happy to help you through this troubling time.

* * *

B. How Can I Help You? Here Are Some Take-Away Techniques from the Example

Here are a few techniques that the attorney used in the prior example:

1. Take-Away Technique #1: The Attorney Stated That He Is There to Help the Client

As the first pillar notes, it is important to let our clients know that we are there to help them. There are many reasons why clients may have misconceptions about what lawyers do—lawyer jokes included. They may think that we are lazy. They may think that we are money-hungry. They may think that we will look down on them. They may think that all we do is argue.

Letting the clients know that we are there to help them with their legal problems can help us begin to help our clients. Yes. There are plenty of helpings to go around. Our job is to help them. They should try to help us. We end up helping each other. This is a professional relationship, but it is still a *relationship*. Like any participant to a successful committed relationship will tell you, both parties to the relationship need to contribute. But, also like any participant to a successful committed relationship will tell you, your actions can speak louder than your words. We can't just tell our clients that we are there to help them. We need to show them as well.

Let's take a look at the next two take-away techniques to see how the attorney from the example *showed* Ms. James that he was there to help her.

2. Take-Away Technique #2: The Attorney Let the Client Know, Early on, That He Was Familiar with the Client's Situation and That He Was Beginning to Understand How the Situation Was Impacting the Client

Letting our clients know that we are somewhat familiar with their cases helps show the clients that they matter. It helps show the clients that they are more than, perhaps, billable hours. It also helps provide an opportunity for the clients to begin to express some thoughts, concerns, or expectations relating to their legal problems.

A client who distrusts attorneys or who is afraid of working with an attorney may be less inclined to want to speak with us if we said something like this:

* * *

Attorney:	Oh, yeah. My 10:00AM appointment. Hi. Umm. I know you are my 10:00AM appointment.
Client:	Yes. Loretta James. I am here for my 10:00AM appointment.
Attorney:	Good. What do you need?

* * *

Or this:

* * *

Attorney:	Hello. It's Ms. James, right?
Client:	Yes. Loretta James.
Attorney:	Listen, I know you are my 10:00AM appointment, but I've got to go. I just got word that an earlier tee time for the golf club is open. I'm sure you understand. Someone else here should be able talk to you.

* * *

A client who distrusts attorneys or who is afraid of working with an attorney may also question how helpful and understanding we might be if the exchange included the following interaction. As you read the exchange, try to identify the positive and negative aspects of the attorney's interaction with Ms. James:

* * *

Attorney:	Thank you for coming in to the office, Ms. James. This is my paralegal, Stacy Garcia. I know you have spent some time speaking with Stacy over the telephone. She will be sitting in on the interview with me today and will help take notes of what is said during the interview.
Client:	Yes. Hello, Stacy.
Paralegal:	Hello, Ms. James.
Attorney:	So, Ms. James. Did you have any trouble finding our office?
Client:	Oh, no. It was easy.
Attorney:	Good. Well, Ms. James, we understand that you are concerned about the letter you received that threatens a lawsuit against you.
Client:	Yes. I received the letter a few days ago, and I have been worrying about it ever since. I have never been sued. I don't know what to do.
Attorney:	Look, Ms. James. We are here to help you. And we have handled many similar cases. Your worries are just silly. So, you should just drop them.

* * *

The first two ineffective examples show an attorney who may appear (or, quite frankly, is) disinterested. A client who distrusts attorneys or who is afraid of working with an attorney is going to be even more distrusting or afraid if she is presented with an attorney from the first two examples.

The attorney in the last example was somewhat more welcoming, and he did identify that Ms. James is upset about being sued. But, he also devalued her feelings when he stated, "Your worries are just silly." The attorney did not make Ms. James believe that he was aware of how troubled she was feeling. Rather, he simply told Ms. James to "drop" whatever concerns she may have been feeling.

The attorney in the last example did not begin to show Ms. James that he understands what she is going through. He did not respect Ms. James' feelings, and he did not empathize. This lack of acknowledgement of the client's thoughts, concerns, or expectations relating to her legal problem can slow down the establishment of rapport. And a lack of rapport can create further obstacles to our effective representation of our clients.

3. *Take-Away Technique #3: The Attorney Allowed the Client to Talk*

I have already discussed the importance of allowing our clients to express some thoughts, concerns, or expectations relating to their legal problems. But, what I have not discussed is that the attorney needs to allow the client to speak.

In a client interview, there is usually a certain time where the client has the floor. The attorney quiets down and allows the client to tell her story. This time usually corresponds to a lot of fact gathering: the attorney listens to the client discuss facts related to the legal problem. The attorney may ask some follow-up questions that may help clarify some of the facts of the case. But, for the most part, the attorney quietly listens and, perhaps, takes notes.

However, we can quiet down and allow the client to speak long before the fact-gathering stage of a client interview. The initial moments of a client interview—especially an initial client interview—can set the tone to the rest of our representation. We can build rapport by letting our clients know that what *they* have to say matters to us. Yes. We are attorneys, and we *really* like to hear ourselves speak. But, our silence can often have a great impact on the professional relationship we build with our clients. As a result of our silence, clients may begin to feel more comfortable *talking to us*. They may feel like they need to fill in that silence with more information. They may begin to open up and express some of their thoughts, concerns, or expectations relating to their legal problems. As a result of our pillar-one work, our clients may begin to realize that what *they have to say* will help us help them.

CHAPTER 8

The Second Pillar—Let the Clients Talk

The second pillar to the conversation foundation is letting the clients talk. Let's examine this pillar a little further.

A. I Am Important. You Are Important. We Are All Important.

Yes. One of the take-away techniques from the prior chapter was that the attorney let the client talk. Let me "talk" a little more about letting the clients talk.

Let's face it. As attorneys, we really do like to speak. And why shouldn't we speak? We have a lot of important stuff to say.

We survived and thrived in the Socratic classrooms. We learned to critically think about the law. And we spent many days applying law to the facts of many cases. We are lawyers. We can advocate. We can negotiate. We can litigate.

So. Yes. What we often have to say can be important. But, what the clients have to say is just as important. We can't effectively advocate for our clients if we don't know what we are advocating for. We can't negotiate a successful settlement for our clients if we don't know what matters most to our clients. And we can't meaningfully litigate a claim if we don't know what the clients say about their claims. So, resist the urge to overtake the client interview. Put a sock in it, and hand over the stage to the clients. You will have an opportunity later in the interview to impress the clients with all your fancy application of the law to the clients' stories. Let the clients tell their stories first.

B. Dealing with Quiet Clients—Opening the Door to a Client's Story

Just because we like to talk, doesn't mean that our clients will freely speak. Yes, there may be times when we wish our clients would just take a breath and quiet down. But, many of our clients will be less inclined to open up and invite us into their respective stories. As the singer/songwriter *Alanis Morissette* might say, we can't just break into a client's story *uninvited*. We can't always expect for our clients to willingly take over the stage and open up about their respective problems. They may be nervous. They may not like us. They may not know what is important for their cases. They may not know what to open up about.

I already spoke about the first pillar to the conversation foundation—letting your clients know that you are there to help them. As I mentioned, this first pillar can help put clients at ease. Letting your clients know that you are there to help them may help to begin to establish rapport. It encourages the clients to consider opening the door and inviting you into their stories.

Let's revisit the Ms. James example. As you read the exchange, try to identify how the interview progresses under the second pillar to the conversation foundation. See if the attorney lets Ms. James talk (the new part of the interview begins after the four arrows):

* * *

Attorney:	Hello, Ms. James. Thank you so much for coming by the office this morning. This is my paralegal, Stacy Garcia. I know you have spent some time speaking with Stacy over the telephone. She will be sitting in on the interview with me today and will help take notes of what is said during the interview.
Client:	Yes. Hello, Stacy.
Paralegal:	Hello, Ms. James.
Attorney:	So, Ms. James. Did you have any trouble finding our office?
Client:	Oh, no. It was easy.
Attorney:	Good. Well, Ms. James, we understand that you have received a letter that states that you are going to be sued in state court.
Client:	Yes. I received the letter a few days ago, and I have been worrying about it ever since. I have never been sued. I don't know what to do.
Attorney:	We understand that this must be very difficult for you, Ms. James. Receiving a letter that threatens a lawsuit against you can be very upsetting—especially if you have never been sued before.

Client:	Yes. It is very upsetting.
Attorney:	Well, the good thing is that you are here today and that you are seeking legal representation. We have handled similar lawsuits before. And we are happy to help you through this troubling time.

→   →   →   →

Client:	Thank you. That is very reassuring. It is good to hear that.
Attorney:	Great. We are glad that you are feeling a little more reassured. Hopefully, the rest of the interview will continue to help lessen some of your concerns.
Client:	Yes. I hope so.
Attorney:	Wonderful. Well, we understand that you are worried about this letter that you received that threatens a lawsuit against you. We'd love to spend some time just letting you tell us a little more about what may have happened that might have led to this potential lawsuit. And as you tell us your story, Ms. James, we'd love for you to be as open and honest as possible. Because the more information that we know about your situation, the better we are able to assist you.
Client:	Yes. Okay.
Attorney:	Great. Well, why don't you tell us what has brought you in today, and how we might be able to help you?

Client:	Well, as the letter notes, I am the owner of *Dressing It Up!* It's a clothing store off of McGregor and Jewel. I started it all on my own. I do some of the designs, and I import some other designs. It has been really great owning my own store, and I have even considered opening up another branch of the store downtown. Well, that's until I received this lawsuit letter. Who knows what will happen now?
Attorney:	Wow, Ms. James! It sounds like you have worked really hard to get your business going. It must be really exciting for you to be able to run your own business. But, this lawsuit letter seems to have dampened some of your excitement a bit. Talk to us a little more about what happened with Mr. Sampson. We understand that he is the gentleman who wrote you the letter.
Client:	Sure. It seems quite silly to me that he is threatening to sue me. You see. Mr. Sampson is somewhat of a regular customer. He gets all of his dress shirts and ties at my store. One day, I was assisting another customer when I saw him walk outside and fall. He took a few steps after exiting the store, and he slipped. Fell right on his backside.
Attorney:	Okay.

Client:	So, it had been raining most of the day. The sidewalk outside the store was a little damp. There were a few puddles. I remember I had told myself I needed to go put a warning sign outside the door—warning that the ground may be slippery. But, I got busy with another customer.
Attorney:	Interesting. So, you saw Mr. Sampson take a few steps outside the store, and fall on his backside. You said that it had been raining prior to the time Mr. Sampson fell. And you recall wanting to put a sign outside the door warning that the ground may be slippery. But, you were not able to do so, because you started attending to another customer. Can you tell me anything else that was going on at the time he fell? For instance, how was the lighting? What was he doing or carrying when he fell?
Client:	Well, I believe that the lighting was fine. It was just after 1:00PM. It was a little cloudy, but it was not like it was dark outside. The skies had cleared up.
Attorney:	Okay.
Client:	Oh! And I remember that he was doing something with his cell phone as he exited the door. Like if he was reading an email or a text or something. He was very fixated on his phone.

* * *

C. Uninvited? Here Are Some Take-Away Techniques from the Example

Here are a couple of techniques that the attorney used in the prior example:

1. *Take-Away Technique #1: The Attorney Didn't Feel Compelled to Force the Client to Speak Right Away*

Notice that the attorney did not push Ms. James to quickly jump into the facts of her case. Even though the attorney knew that he could not advise Ms. James on her impending lawsuit without the facts of the case, he allowed for some additional back-and-forth conversation before asking for her story. This extra time provided the attorney another opportunity to acknowledge Ms. James' concerns about the lawsuit, which likely helped to continue to establish rapport.

Let's revisit the exchange between the attorney and Ms. James. As you read the exchange, try to identify where the attorney is helping to build trust and rapport with Ms. James. Try to also identify where the attorney loses some of this trust and rapport (the new part of the interview begins after the four arrows):

* * *

Attorney:	Hello, Ms. James. Thank you so much for coming by the office this morning. This is my paralegal, Stacy Garcia. I know you have spent some time speaking with Stacy over the telephone. She will be sitting in on the interview with me today and will help take notes of what is said during the interview.
Client:	Yes. Hello, Stacy.
Paralegal:	Hello, Ms. James.
Attorney:	So, Ms. James. Did you have any trouble finding our office?
Client:	Oh, no. It was easy.
Attorney:	Good. Well, Ms. James, we understand that you have received a letter that states that you are going to be sued in state court.
Client:	Yes. I received the letter a few days ago, and I have been worrying about it ever since. I have never been sued. I don't know what to do.
Attorney:	We understand that this must be very difficult for you, Ms. James. Receiving a letter that threatens a lawsuit against you can be very upsetting—especially if you have never been sued before.
Client:	Yes. It is very upsetting.
Attorney:	Well, the good thing is that you are here today and that you are seeking legal representation. We have handled similar lawsuits before. And we are happy to help you through this troubling time.

Client:	Thank you. That is very reassuring. It is good to hear that.
→ → → →	
Attorney:	Well, it appears that the letter claims that you and your store caused Mr. Sampson to fall and sustain a bunch of injuries. Is that true?
Client:	Well, no. I mean. Yes. I mean. I am the owner of the store, and Mr. Sampson did fall. But, I did not cause the accident. At least, I don't think I did.

* * *

In the above example, the attorney began the exchange with some helpful building of trust and rapport. The attorney acknowledged some of Ms. James' concerns about the lawsuit, and he noted that he was happy to help her through her "troubling time."

However, the attorney lost some trust and rapport during the latter part of the exchange. Towards the end of the exchange, the attorney neglected to acknowledge that Ms. James was feeling somewhat reassured. Ms. James had already stated that she had never been sued before and that she was quite worried about the lawsuit. She also indicated that she was feeling a little reassured based on the initial conversation with the attorney.

Instead of using this slight opening of the door to further establish rapport with Ms. James, the attorney put the client on the defense right at the start of the interview—especially with his "Is that true?" lawyerly question.

The attorney likely erased any reassurance that might have been established with Ms. James, which may have further confused her. He likely made Ms. James feel even more anxious than she was when she walked into the office. He likely shut the door closed even before Ms. James was able to say anything relevant about the lawsuit. He may have helped scratch himself off the invited guest list.

a.   Additional Tip #1: Pay Attention to the Signals the Clients Present to You!

As attorneys, we can make our jobs more difficult by simply not following some of the signals that the clients present to us. In the last example, Ms. James' signal was a direct verbal statement that she was feeling a little better than the way she was feeling when she walked into the office.

Now, I know some of you are probably saying that you are not equipped to deal with the clients' *feelings* (or, the "F" word, as some attorneys may think). But, we don't have to be all "touchy-feely" to be able to identify and acknowledge our clients' feelings. We don't have to have any special training in counseling. And, we don't have to have gone through therapy ourselves. We just have to be able to pay attention. And we have to understand that we are not the only important party to this relationship. Let the client know that she is just as important to the relationship. Continue to build trust and rapport.

Here are a few ways that the attorney could have quickly, but effectively, acknowledged what Ms. James had said about feeling a little better than the way she was feeling when she walked into the office:

• "That is good to hear."

- "Wonderful."

- "We are so happy to hear that."

b.   Additional Tip #2: It's Not Only What You Say, but Also How You Say It! Turn the "Caps Lock" Off!

I mentioned earlier that you don't have to be an *Oscar*-winning actor to effectively converse with your client. But, as I also mentioned earlier, the tone of your voice does have a large impact on how you come across to your client. You are less likely to build trust and rapport with your client if your tone is the equivalent of an email or text IN ALL CAPS.

Imagine the three examples from above in all capital letters:

- "THAT IS GOOD TO HEAR."

- "WONDERFUL."

- "WE ARE SO HAPPY TO HEAR THAT."

THERE IS JUST SOMETHING ABOUT READING A TEXT IN ALL CAPITAL LETTERS. OH! Sorry. There is just something about reading a text in all capital letters. Even though the sender may not have intended to type a message to us in all caps, we receive and interpret the message within the context of how the message was presented to us. As a result, we may be somewhat suspicious or confused about what was said. We may not believe what was said. Or, we may proceed in the conversation with extra precaution.

The same rings true with our verbal conversations with our clients. We want to establish trust and rapport. We want our clients to believe us. We don't want them to misinterpret what we say. We want them to be as open and honest as they can be with us, so that we have the necessary information to help solve their problems. So, we should watch our tone of voice when we speak with our clients. Let's try to make sure that our "Caps Lock" is off.

c.   Additional Tip #3: It's Not Only What You Say, but Also How You Say It! Watch Your Emoji!

Let's take the tone of voice tip to another level: emoji. Now, don't act like you have never used one. Admit it. We all have attached a "happy" face emoji to an email or text message at one point in our lives.

So, imagine this. An adult of a certain age tells his child that he did not have text messages when he was growing up. The child replies back with a picture of an "astonished" or "crying" face emoji. Here, the emoji sets the tone to what the child wants to say.

Now, consider the three examples from above with emoji that don't represent what we are really trying to say or how we want to say it:

- "That is good to hear" (with a "sleeping" face emoji).
- "Wonderful" (with a "smirking" face emoji).
- "We are so happy to hear that" (with a "neutral" or "unamused" face emoji).

I know it may seem silly to discuss emoji in the context of an attorney-client interview. After all, this is a professional relationship. And we are not physically attaching emoji to our conversations with our clients. Are we?

Well, the tone of our voice and our nonverbal communication with our clients essentially act as emoji. They provide context to what we are trying to say to our clients. And much like the recipient of an all caps text message, our clients can be discouraged to continue with our conversation if our tone of voice and nonverbal communications don't match up with what we are trying to say.

We don't want to appear to be unamused when we say something like "We are so happy to hear that." We don't want to come across as sarcastic if we really think it is "wonderful" that the client is feeling reassured. So, make sure you marry what you say and mean with appropriate tone of voice and nonverbal communication. Try to "attach" a fitting emoji to your conversations with your clients.

Now, let's get back to the take-away techniques from the previous Ms. James example.

2. Take-Away Technique #2: The Attorney Used Open-Ended Questions to Help Encourage the Client to Tell Her Story

We likely have all received an email or text message that was sent in all capital letters. As I mentioned earlier, there is just something about those types of messages that tends to be off-putting. We often feel offended. We shut down. We don't reply to the message. Or, if we do, the reply is relatively short. We can similarly shut down a client interview by primarily using closed-ended questions at the start of the interview.

Closed-ended questions are those that only require a relatively short answer. They don't really encourage the client to answer with an explanation. They only encourage a one or two word answer—usually only a "yes" or "no" answer.

Let's take another look at the effective exchange with Ms. James. As you read the exchange, try to identify how the attorney used open-ended questions to encourage Ms. James to tell her story:

* * *

Attorney:	Hello, Ms. James. Thank you so much for coming by the office this morning. This is my paralegal, Stacy Garcia. I know you have spent some time speaking with Stacy over the telephone. She will be sitting in on the interview with me today and will help take notes of what is said during the interview.
Client:	Yes. Hello, Stacy.
Paralegal:	Hello, Ms. James.
Attorney:	So, Ms. James. Did you have any trouble finding our office?
Client:	Oh, no. It was easy.
Attorney:	Good. Well, Ms. James, we understand that you have received a letter that states that you are going to be sued in state court.
Client:	Yes. I received the letter a few days ago, and I have been worrying about it ever since. I have never been sued. I don't know what to do.
Attorney:	We understand that this must be very difficult for you, Ms. James. Receiving a letter that threatens a lawsuit against you can be very upsetting—especially if you have never been sued before.
Client:	Yes. It is very upsetting.

Attorney:	Well, the good thing is that you are here today and that you are seeking legal representation. We have handled similar lawsuits before. And we are happy to help you through this troubling time.
Client:	Thank you. That is very reassuring. It is good to hear that.
Attorney:	Great. We are glad that you are feeling a little more reassured. Hopefully, the rest of the interview will continue to help lessen some of your concerns.
Client:	Yes. I hope so.
Attorney:	Wonderful. Well, we understand that you are worried about this letter that you received that threatens a lawsuit against you. We'd love to spend some time just letting you tell us a little more about what may have happened that might have led to this potential lawsuit. And as you tell us your story, Ms. James, we'd love for you to be as open and honest as possible. Because the more information that we know about your situation, the better we are able to assist you.
Client:	Yes. Okay.
Attorney:	Great. Well, why don't you tell us what has brought you in today, and how we might be able to help you?
Client:	Well, as the letter notes, I am the owner of *Dressing It Up!* It's a clothing store off of McGregor and Jewel. I started it all on my own. I

do some of the designs, and I import some other designs. It has been really great owning my own store, and I have even considered opening up another branch of the store downtown. Well, that's until I received this lawsuit letter. Who knows what will happen now?

Attorney: Wow, Ms. James! It sounds like you have worked really hard to get your business going. It must be really exciting for you to be able to run your own business. But, this lawsuit letter seems to have dampened some of your excitement a bit. Talk to us a little more about what happened with Mr. Sampson. We understand that he is the gentleman who wrote you the letter.

Client: Sure. It seems quite silly to me that he is threatening to sue me. You see, Mr. Sampson is somewhat of a regular customer. He gets all of his dress shirts and ties at my store. One day, I was assisting another customer when I saw him walk outside and fall. He took a few steps after exiting the store, and he slipped. Fell right on his backside.

Attorney: Okay.

Client: So, it had been raining most of the day. The sidewalk outside the store was a little damp. There were a few puddles. I remember I had told myself I needed to go put a warning sign outside the door—warning that the ground may

	be slippery. But, I got busy with another customer.
Attorney:	Interesting. So, you saw Mr. Sampson take a few steps outside the store, and fall on his backside. You said that it had been raining prior to the time Mr. Sampson fell. And you recall wanting to put a sign outside the door warning that the ground may be slippery. But, you were not able to do so, because you started attending to another customer. Can you tell me anything else that was going on at the time he fell? For instance, how was the lighting? What was he doing or carrying when he fell?
Client:	Well, I believe that the lighting was fine. It was just after 1:00PM. It was a little cloudy, but it was not like it was dark outside. The skies had cleared up.
Attorney:	Okay.
Client:	Oh! And I remember that he was doing something with his cell phone as he exited the door. Like if he was reading an email or a text or something. He was very fixated on his phone.

* * *

Notice that the attorney in this effective example began with a few open-ended questions to facilitate the start of Ms. James' story:

- "Well, why don't you tell us what has brought you in today, and how we might be able to help you?"

- "Talk to us a little more about what happened with Mr. Sampson. We understand that he is the gentleman who wrote you the letter."

- "Can you tell me anything else that was going on at the time he fell? For instance, how was the lighting? What was he doing or carrying when he fell?"

These questions told Ms. James that she had the stage. They told her that she could speak about whatever she felt might be relevant to the lawsuit. They showed her that what she had to say about the lawsuit mattered.

Asking closed-ended questions, particularly at the start of the client interview, can "close" off a lot of what our clients could or would say. If part of our job as problem solvers is to understand how the relevant law applies to our clients' stories, we need to encourage our clients to tell their stories. Open-ended questions provide a channel for this encouragement.

Let's look at another possible exchange with Ms. James. As you read the exchange, try to identify how a close-ended question can shut down a lot of the client's story (the new part of the interview begins after the four arrows):

* * *

Attorney:	Well, the good thing is that you are here today and that you are seeking legal representation. We have handled similar lawsuits before. And we are happy to help you through this troubling

	time.
Client:	Thank you. That is very reassuring. It is good to hear that.

→   →   →   →

Attorney:	Great. Well, it appears that the letter claims that you and your store caused Mr. Sampson to fall and sustain a bunch of injuries.
Client:	Yes. I believe that is what the letter says.
Attorney:	Well, this is the typical premises liability case. Or, as some people sometimes say—your typical slip and fall case. And like I said, our firm has handled many slip and fall cases. In these types of cases, there is usually some liability on the business owner if the owner was aware of some potential problem at the store, and did not fix it or warn about it. In other words, say Mr. Sampson slipped on a spilled soda inside your store. And say you were aware of the spilled soda, and did not clean it up or warn customers that the floor was slippery. Then you'd likely have some liability for the accident. Did anything like this happen? Were you aware of anything wrong with the store that might have led to Mr. Sampson falling down?
Client:	Well, yes. It had been raining on the day he fell. I wanted to put a slippery warning sign outside the door, but I didn't.

Attorney:	Oh, that's too bad. So, you were aware that it was slippery outside, and you did nothing. That's going to make things really difficult for us.
Client:	Oh. Okay.
Attorney:	So, we will need to start thinking about his injuries and what kind of damages he can recover.

* * *

There are at least two concerns going on in this ineffective example, and we will get to the second concern in Subpart 3 below. But since this subpart heading identified the use of open-ended questions, let's tackle that one first.

In this example, the attorney's first substantive questions to the client were close-ended questions. The attorney did not encourage any explanatory responses from Ms. James. And his failure to start off with open-ended questions severely limited the focus of Ms. James' story. Let's take another look at the attorney's questions:

- "Did anything like this happen?"
- "Were you aware of anything wrong with the store that might have led to Mr. Sampson falling down?"

These questions told Ms. James that the attorney only wanted to hear a short "yes" or "no" response. The questions did not encourage Ms. James to explain why she may not have put the warning sign out—the questions just presumed that she was at fault for not doing so.

The questions also limited the focus of what Ms. James could have told the attorney. They told Ms. James that it did not matter what Mr. Sampson may have been doing at the time he slipped and fell. Ms. James may later forget to tell the attorney that Mr. Sampson's cell phone may have distracted him at the time he fell. Or, she may assume that this fact is not important to her story, since the attorney did not *specifically* ask her if Mr. Sampson was distracted by his cell phone at the time he fell.

By starting the interview with close-ended questions, the attorney essentially highlighted to Ms. James what the relevant facts of the case should be—even before hearing any facts from her story! Yes, the attorney may have later discovered that Mr. Sampson's cell phone distracted him at the time he fell. The attorney may end up cleaning up some of this "mess." But as any parent who has had to clean up a child's spilled glass of milk will tell you, why not try to avoid the mess in the first place? Put a lid on that cup, and start off with some open-ended questions.

3. Take-Away Technique #3: The Attorney Resisted the Urge to Speak and Allowed the Client to Take the Stage

I mentioned that there were at least two concerns with the above ineffective conversation with Ms. James. As I mentioned, the first concern is that the attorney asked closed-ended questions to start the client interview. The second concern with the ineffective conversation is that the attorney did not resist the urge to speak.

Let's take another look at the ineffective example. As you read the exchange, try to identify where the attorney could have resisted the urge to speak:

* * *

Attorney:	Well, the good thing is that you are here today and that you are seeking legal representation. We have handled similar lawsuits before. And we are happy to help you through this troubling time.
Client:	Thank you. That is very reassuring. It is good to hear that.
Attorney:	Great. Well, it appears that the letter claims that you and your store caused Mr. Sampson to fall and sustain a bunch of injuries.
Client:	Yes. I believe that is what the letter says.
Attorney:	Well, this is the typical premises liability case. Or, as some people sometimes say—your typical slip and fall case. And like I said, our firm has handled many slip and fall cases. In these types of cases, there is usually some liability on the business owner if the owner was aware of some potential problem at the store, and did not fix it or warn about it. In other words, say Mr. Sampson slipped on a spilled soda inside your store. And say you were aware of the spilled soda, and did not clean it up or warn customers that the floor was slippery. Then you'd likely have some liability for the accident. Did anything like this happen? Were you aware of anything wrong with the store that might have led to Mr. Sampson falling down?

Client:	Well, yes. It had been raining on the day he fell. I wanted to put a slippery warning sign outside the door, but I didn't.
Attorney:	Oh, that's too bad. So, you were aware that it was slippery outside, and you did nothing. That's going to make things really difficult for us.
Client:	Oh. Okay.
Attorney:	So, we will need to start thinking about his injuries and what kind of damages he can recover.

* * *

Notice that, in addition to starting the fact-gathering portion of the interview with some close-ended questions, the attorney never really handed over the stage to Ms. James. He did not give Ms. James an opportunity to tell her story. He did not show Ms. James that what *she* has to say is important. He only made it seem like his words are the words that matter. He hogged the stage and immediately began setting out the law for the case and his evaluation of the case—even before fully understanding what happened at the time Mr. Sampson slipped and fell!

Compare the ineffective example with the effective example from Part B of this chapter. You will notice that a major difference between the two examples is that the attorney let Ms. James talk in the *effective* example. The attorney encouraged Ms. James to tell her story, AND *he allowed Ms. James to tell her story*. He didn't start spouting premises liability law like a water sprinkler and applying this law to facts that he did not even know existed.

Legal research and writing faculty will tell you that you shouldn't start applying the law to the facts of your case in the legal documents that you write until you have fully explained the law. Well, you can't start applying the law to the facts of your case if you never get any facts from the client to begin with. Yes, our clients will have many questions for us during the interview. And, yes. They will want answers to these questions very quickly. But, we won't impress them by trying to solve their legal problems before they have had an opportunity to describe their legal problems. And they won't be particularly thrilled when our answers are unsatisfactory or incomplete. So, before we try to answer some of their most pressing questions—before we take command of the stage and explain the law—try to get the clients to speak. I am sure you have a really nice voice. And I am sure that you speak quite eloquently. But, resist the urge to speak. And hand the stage over to the client first.

CHAPTER 9

The Third Pillar— Listen!

The third pillar to the conversation foundation is listening to our clients. Listen up, as we talk a little more about listening.

A. We Are Not Like *Charlie Brown*

Our job does not stop after our clients begin to tell us their stories. We can't spend so much time establishing rapport and encouraging our clients to tell their stories, then forget to spend some time listening to the stories.

Listening is harder than you think. Or, I should say that listening *correctly* is harder than you think. Listening is more than simply sitting near the client and hearing random noises coming from the client's mouth. No. We are not in a *Peanuts* cartoon. We can't effectively represent our clients if all we hear from our clients is "blah-blah, blah-blah, blah-blah, blah-blah."

B. Have You Stretched? It's Active Listening Time

I said that listening correctly is a difficult task. And when I say, "listening correctly," I mean active listening. Are you hearing me? You've got to practice active listening when you are listening to your clients' stories.

Mental health professionals practice active listening every day. Active listening is a counseling technique where the mental health professional listens to what the client is saying and tries to understand the client's perspective. The mental health professional not only listens to the facts associated with the client's story, but she listens to any goals, values, and feelings that might be attached to the client's story. After the client has told her story, the mental health professional reflects back to the client what the client said *and* how the professional understands what the client is going through. Active listening helps promote trust and rapport. It shows the client that what she *says, feels, and values* matter.

Attorneys should also actively listen to their clients— especially during an initial client interview. We can't expect to effectively represent our clients if we just passively listen to the stories that our clients present to us. We need to be present, in mind and body, while the clients tell us their stories. We need to keenly listen to the facts that the clients discuss. We need to pay attention to what our clients say and how they say it, as well as what they don't say. We need to identify any feelings or values that the clients may attach to their stories. And we need to be prepared to reflect back to the clients what they have just told and presented to us. We need to continue to build that trust and rapport.

Yes. This seems like a lot of work. It is a lot of work. When we actively listen, we are listening not only to the facts that might potentially be relevant to the case. We are also listening to any body language or other nonverbal behavior that the clients display as they tell us their stories. We are also listening for any goals, values, and emotions that the clients present that might help paint a better picture of the clients' perspectives on their legal problems.

Let's revisit the complete effective exchange between the attorney and Ms. James in the slip and fall hypothetical. As you read the exchange, see if you can identify where the attorney is practicing active listening (the new part of the interview begins after the four arrows):

* * *

Attorney:	Hello, Ms. James. Thank you so much for coming by the office this morning. This is my paralegal, Stacy Garcia. I know you have spent some time speaking with Stacy over the telephone. She will be sitting in on the interview with me today and will help take notes of what is said during the interview.
Client:	Yes. Hello, Stacy.
Paralegal:	Hello, Ms. James.
Attorney:	So, Ms. James. Did you have any trouble finding our office?
Client:	Oh, no. It was easy.

Attorney:	Good. Well, Ms. James, we understand that you have received a letter that states that you are going to be sued in state court.
Client:	Yes. I received the letter a few days ago, and I have been worrying about it ever since. I have never been sued. I don't know what to do.
Attorney:	We understand that this must be very difficult for you, Ms. James. Receiving a letter that threatens a lawsuit against you can be very upsetting—especially if you have never been sued before.
Client:	Yes. It is very upsetting.
Attorney:	Well, the good thing is that you are here today and that you are seeking legal representation. We have handled similar lawsuits before. And we are happy to help you through this troubling time.
Client:	Thank you. That is very reassuring. It is good to hear that.
Attorney:	Great. We are glad that you are feeling a little more reassured. Hopefully, the rest of the interview will continue to help lessen some of your concerns.
Client:	Yes. I hope so.
Attorney:	Wonderful. Well, we understand that you are worried about this letter that you received that threatens a lawsuit against you. We'd love to spend some time just letting you tell us a little

	more about what may have happened that might have led to this potential lawsuit. And as you tell us your story, Ms. James, we'd love for you to be as open and honest as possible. Because the more information that we know about your situation, the better we are able to assist you.
Client:	Yes. Okay.
Attorney:	Great. Well, why don't you tell us what has brought you in today, and how we might be able to help you?
Client:	Well, as the letter notes, I am the owner of *Dressing It Up!* It's a clothing store off of McGregor and Jewel. I started it all on my own. I do some of the designs, and I import some other designs. It has been really great owning my own store, and I have even considered opening up another branch of the store downtown. Well, that's until I received this lawsuit letter. Who knows what will happen now?
Attorney:	Wow, Ms. James! It sounds like you have worked really hard to get your business going. It must be really exciting for you to be able to run your own business. But, this lawsuit letter seems to have dampened some of your excitement a bit. Talk to us a little more about what happened with Mr. Sampson. We understand that he is the gentleman who wrote you the letter.

Client:	Sure. It seems quite silly to me that he is threatening to sue me. You see. Mr. Sampson is somewhat of a regular customer. He gets all of his dress shirts and ties at my store. One day, I was assisting another customer when I saw him walk outside and fall. He took a few steps after exiting the store, and he slipped. Fell right on his backside.
Attorney:	Okay.
Client:	So, it had been raining most of the day. The sidewalk outside the store was a little damp. There were a few puddles. I remember I had told myself I needed to go put a warning sign outside the door—warning that the ground may be slippery. But, I got busy with another customer.
Attorney:	Interesting. So, you saw Mr. Sampson take a few steps outside the store, and fall on his backside. You said that it had been raining prior to the time Mr. Sampson fell. And you recall wanting to put a sign outside the door warning that the ground may be slippery. But, you were not able to do so, because you started attending to another customer. Can you tell me anything else that was going on at the time he fell? For instance, how was the lighting? What was he doing or carrying when he fell?

Client:	Well, I believe that the lighting was fine. It was just after 1:00PM. It was a little cloudy, but it was not like it was dark outside. The skies had cleared up.
Attorney:	Okay.
Client:	Oh! And I remember that he was doing something with his cell phone as he exited the door. Like if he was reading an email or a text or something. He was very fixated on his phone.
→ → → →	
Attorney:	Okay. Thank you for sharing that with us, Ms. James.
Client:	Oh. Okay. Well, you are welcome.
Attorney:	So, it sounds like the day that Mr. Sampson fell was a pretty normal day at your business. Although it had rained earlier in the day, the sky had cleared up. And there did not appear to be any lighting issues whereby Mr. Sampson would have been unable to see because it was too dark or there was some type of light bulb missing.
Client:	Right.
Attorney:	But, there may have been something preventing Mr. Sampson from fully seeing the rainy sidewalk outside your store. You do remember seeing Mr. Sampson as he exited the store, and it looked to you like he was doing

> something on his cell phone. Like reading an
> email or a text message.
>
> Client: Yes.

* * *

C. Listen Up! Here Are Some Take-Away Techniques from the Example

Here are a few active listening techniques that the attorney used in the prior example:

1. *Take-Away Technique #1: The Attorney Reflected Back to the Client the Content of the Client's Message*

Notice how the attorney repeated back to Ms. James some of the factual information that she stated. This type of summarization by the attorney of the factual information that the client discusses with us is called reflection. By reflecting back to our clients the content of the clients' stories, we can show our clients that we have been listening to the details surrounding their problems. We can show that we are beginning to gain an understanding of the important facts related to their stories. And if we don't fully gain an understanding of the facts, we can ask clarifying questions along with our reflection of the content to help clear things up. We can also ask our clients to correct any information that we may have misunderstood or misstated.

Let's take a look at one instance where the attorney reflects back to Ms. James some of the content from her story. Notice how the attorney paraphrases some of the factual information that Ms. James presented to him:

* * *

Client:	So, it had been raining most of the day. The sidewalk outside the store was a little damp. There were a few puddles. I remember I had told myself I needed to go put a warning sign outside the door—warning that the ground may be slippery. But, I got busy with another customer.
Attorney:	Interesting. So, you saw Mr. Sampson take a few steps outside the store, and fall on his backside. You said that it had been raining prior to the time Mr. Sampson fell. And you recall wanting to put a sign outside the door warning that the ground may be slippery. But, you were not able to do so, because you started attending to another customer. Can you tell me anything else that was going on at the time he fell? For instance, how was the lighting? What was he doing or carrying when he fell?

* * *

Here's another example of the attorney's reflection of the factual content that Ms. James presented:

* * *

Attorney:	So, it sounds like the day that Mr. Sampson fell was a pretty normal day at your business. Although it had rained earlier in the day, the sky had cleared up. And there did not appear to be any lighting issues whereby Mr. Sampson would have been unable to see because it was too dark or there was some type of light bulb missing.
Client:	Right.
Attorney:	But, there may have been something preventing Mr. Sampson from fully seeing the rainy sidewalk outside your store. You do remember seeing Mr. Sampson as he exited the store, and it looked to you like he was doing something on his cell phone. Like reading an email or a text message.
Client:	Yes.

* * *

Both effective examples above show the attorney summarizing some of the content relating to what Ms. James just told him and his paralegal. The attorney didn't worry about restating everything Ms. James said word-for-word. He simply paraphrased some of the facts that she told them during the interview. These paraphrased facts may begin to set the foundation to what the attorney feels are the more relevant facts for the case.

Notice also how the attorney used some clarifying questions in the first example. He reflected back to Ms. James some of the content relating to the weather conditions and the warning sign that she wanted to put outside the door. But, he also ended his reflection with a few direct questions to Ms. James that likely helped fill in the gap to Ms. James' story. Asking clarifying questions is a good way to help focus our clients on aspects of their stories that we have not fully understood.

2. *Take-Away Technique #2: The Attorney Reflected Back to the Client the Values and Emotions Attached to the Content of the Story*

In addition to reflecting back the content of Ms. James' story, notice how the attorney also repeated back to Ms. James some of the values and emotions that were attached to her story. This type of reflection is very important in active listening. It shows our clients that we not only understand *what factually happened*, but that we are gaining an understanding of *how the client feels* about what happened as well. It shows our clients that we are getting a better picture about who they are and what matters most to them. It sets the stage for empathy.

Let's take a look at some of the attorney's reflection of the values and emotions attached to Ms. James' story. As you read the examples, see if you can identify what value or emotion the attorney is reflecting back to Ms. James. Here's one example:

* * *

Client:	Yes. I received the letter a few days ago, and I have been worrying about it ever since. I have never been sued. I don't know what to do.

> Attorney: We understand that this must be very difficult for you, Ms. James. Receiving a letter that threatens a lawsuit against you can be very upsetting—especially if you have never been sued before.
>
> Client: Yes. It is very upsetting.
>
> Attorney: Well, the good thing is that you are here today and that you are seeking legal representation. We have handled similar lawsuits before. And we are happy to help you through this troubling time.

* * *

Here's another example:

* * *

> Client: Well, as the letter notes, I am the owner of *Dressing It Up!* It's a clothing store off of McGregor and Jewel. I started it all on my own. I do some of the designs, and I import some other designs. It has been really great owning my own store, and I have even considered opening up another branch of the store downtown. Well, that's until I received this lawsuit letter. Who knows what will happen now?
>
> Attorney: Wow, Ms. James! It sounds like you have worked really hard to get your business going.

> It must be really exciting for you to be able to run your own business. But, this lawsuit letter seems to have dampened some of your excitement a bit. Talk to us a little more about what happened with Mr. Sampson. We understand that he is the gentleman who wrote you the letter.

* * *

In both effective examples above, the attorney identified some value or emotion that Ms. James had either directly or indirectly stated during the conversation. The attorney then reflected back to Ms. James the values or emotions attached to her story, which she acknowledged and appeared to appreciate. This further establishes trust and rapport. This further encourages the clients to open up and help us in helping them solve their problems. Subpart 3 below provides additional discussion relating to the attorney's reflection from these two examples.

3. *Take-Away Technique #3: The Attorney Used His Reflection to Help Move the Client Interview*

The third pillar to the conversation foundation asks that we listen to our clients. Let's take a closer look at two specific instances where the attorney listened as Ms. James identified some value or emotion (these two instances relate to the examples from Subpart 2 above). As you read the exchange, consider the attorney's motivation in wanting to reflect back to the client some of her values and emotions. Consider also how the attorney's reflection helps move the client interview along.

- Ms. James stated that it had been "really great" owning her clothing store.

The attorney heard Ms. James' statement and used his reflection to let her know that *he understands* how excited she is to be a business owner. He reflected back: "Wow, Ms. James! It sounds like you have worked really hard to get your business going. It must be really exciting for you to be able to run your own business."

The attorney also used this reflection to let Ms. James know that he recognizes how much she values her store. This value identification may help the attorney later, either in the interview or in the defense of the case. At some point, the attorney and Ms. James will begin to discuss possible solutions ("legal" and "non-legal") to her problem. Identifying and understanding some of Ms. James' values may help in the exploration of these possible solutions. You will read more about discussing possible "legal" and "non-legal" solutions with your clients in Chapter 16 of the book.

- Ms. James also stated that she has been "worrying" about the potential lawsuit, and that she has "never been sued" and doesn't know what to do.

The attorney heard Ms. James' statements and used his reflection to let her know that *he understands* that she is upset. He reflected back: "We understand that this must be very difficult for you, Ms. James. Receiving a letter that threatens a lawsuit against you can be very upsetting—especially if you have never been sued before."

The attorney also used this reflection of Ms. James' emotion to again let her know that he is there to help her. Here, instead of asking a clarifying question, the attorney used his reflection as a way to transition back to the problem-solving aspect of their professional relationship. He noted: "Well, the good thing is that you are here today and that you are seeking legal representation. We have handled similar lawsuits before. And we are happy to help you through this troubling time." As the extended portion of the exchange demonstrated, the attorney's reflection helped reassure Ms. James that the attorney was really there to help her. She felt comforted. And she felt comfortable in further opening up and telling her story. The attorney then followed the third pillar to the conversation foundation and listened as the client told her story. You will see how the attorney follows the fourth pillar to the conversation foundation in Chapter 10.

The Fourth Pillar—Try to Understand the Clients' Stories

The fourth pillar to the conversation foundation is trying to understand the clients' stories.

Yes. Part of the goal of reflection is showing the clients that we understand what they have told us. The fourth pillar goes beyond just showing the clients that we understand *what they told us*. The fourth pillar shows the clients that we understand *them*.

A. Do You Understand Me? You've Got to Try to Understand the Client's Story!

Remember when I compared client interviews to one of our grade school math word problems? I noted that the information that was presented to you in a word problem was the crucial information that you needed to help find an answer to the word problem. Well, as attorneys, the crucial information that we need that will help us find an answer to our clients' problems comes from the stories that our clients tell us during our client interviews. Part of our job as attorneys *and* counselors requires us to understand our clients' stories.

B.   Pity the Fool Who Does Not Show Empathy!

We have already discussed the importance of establishing trust and rapport. We have discussed strategies to help encourage our clients to open up and tell us their stories. Now that we have worked so hard to get the clients to tell us their stories, we need to try to *understand* their stories. We need to empathize with what the clients are going through.

When our clients tell us their stories, they present us with the information that will help guide our legal analysis. Yes. We might not really know what the relevant law is for our clients' cases without understanding what the cases are really about. So, yes, we need to understand the facts relating to the cases. These facts are important. We will ultimately apply the relevant law to most of these facts when we prosecute or defend our cases. This application will help us explore possible "legal" and "non-legal" solutions to our clients' problems.

But, we also need to understand what is important to our clients. What do they value? What do they want out of their cases? Is it money? Respect? Acceptance? Control? Happiness? Accountability?

There are so many values that the clients can directly or indirectly present to us in their stories. These values often influence the goals and expectations that our clients have that relate to their legal problems. Let's revisit the Ms. James example and see if we can understand her story. Warning: This exchange is quite lengthy. The entire version of the effective conversation up to this point is provided so that you can take notes on what matters most to Ms. James. As you read the exchange, see if you can identify some of the values that Ms. James possesses and how these values may impact her perception of the case (the new part of the interview begins after the four arrows):

* * *

Attorney:	Hello, Ms. James. Thank you so much for coming by the office this morning. This is my paralegal, Stacy Garcia. I know you have spent some time speaking with Stacy over the telephone. She will be sitting in on the interview with me today and will help take notes of what is said during the interview.
Client:	Yes. Hello, Stacy.
Paralegal:	Hello, Ms. James.
Attorney:	So, Ms. James. Did you have any trouble finding our office?
Client:	Oh, no. It was easy.
Attorney:	Good. Well, Ms. James, we understand that you have received a letter that states that you are going to be sued in state court.
Client:	Yes. I received the letter a few days ago, and I have been worrying about it ever since. I have never been sued. I don't know what to do.
Attorney:	We understand that this must be very difficult for you, Ms. James. Receiving a letter that threatens a lawsuit against you can be very upsetting— especially if you have never been sued before.

Client:	Yes. It is very upsetting.
Attorney:	Well, the good thing is that you are here today and that you are seeking legal representation. We have handled similar lawsuits before. And we are happy to help you through this troubling time.
Client:	Thank you. That is very reassuring. It is good to hear that.
Attorney:	Great. We are glad that you are feeling a little more reassured. Hopefully, the rest of the interview will continue to help lessen some of your concerns.
Client:	Yes. I hope so.
Attorney:	Wonderful. Well, we understand that you are worried about this letter that you received that threatens a lawsuit against you. We'd love to spend some time just letting you tell us a little more about what may have happened that might have led to this potential lawsuit. And as you tell us your story, Ms. James, we'd love for you to be as open and honest as possible. Because the more information that we know about your situation, the better we are able to assist you.
Client:	Yes. Okay.
Attorney:	Great. Well, why don't you tell us what has brought you in today, and how we might be able to help you?

Client:	Well, as the letter notes, I am the owner of *Dressing It Up!* It's a clothing store off of McGregor and Jewel. I started it all on my own. I do some of the designs, and I import some other designs. It has been really great owning my own store, and I have even considered opening up another branch of the store downtown. Well, that's until I received this lawsuit letter. Who knows what will happen now?
Attorney:	Wow, Ms. James! It sounds like you have worked really hard to get your business going. It must be really exciting for you to be able to run your own business. But, this lawsuit letter seems to have dampened some of your excitement a bit. Talk to us a little more about what happened with Mr. Sampson. We understand that he is the gentleman who wrote you the letter.
Client:	Sure. It seems quite silly to me that he is threatening to sue me. You see. Mr. Sampson is somewhat of a regular customer. He gets all of his dress shirts and ties at my store. One day, I was assisting another customer when I saw him walk outside and fall. He took a few steps after exiting the store, and he slipped. Fell right on his backside.
Attorney:	Okay.

Client:	So, it had been raining most of the day. The sidewalk outside the store was a little damp. There were a few puddles. I remember I had told myself I needed to go put a warning sign outside the door—warning that the ground may be slippery. But, I got busy with another customer.
Attorney:	Interesting. So, you saw Mr. Sampson take a few steps outside the store, and fall on his backside. You said that it had been raining prior to the time Mr. Sampson fell. And you recall wanting to put a sign outside the door warning that the ground may be slippery. But, you were not able to do so, because you started attending to another customer. Can you tell me anything else that was going on at the time he fell? For instance, how was the lighting? What was he doing or carrying when he fell?
Client:	Well, I believe that the lighting was fine. It was just after 1:00PM. It was a little cloudy, but it was not like it was dark outside. The skies had cleared up.
Attorney:	Okay.
Client:	Oh! And I remember that he was doing something with his cell phone as he exited the door. Like if he was reading an email or a text or something. He was very fixated on his phone.

Attorney:	Okay. Thank you for sharing that with us, Ms. James. So, it sounds like the day that Mr. Sampson fell was a pretty normal day at your business. Although it had rained earlier in the day, the sky had cleared up. And there did not appear to be any lighting issues whereby Mr. Sampson would have been unable to see because it was too dark or there was some type of light bulb missing.
Client:	Right.
Attorney:	But, there may have been something preventing Mr. Sampson from fully seeing the rainy sidewalk outside your store. You do remember seeing Mr. Sampson as he exited the store, and it looked to you like he was doing something on his cell phone. Like reading an email or a text message.
Client:	Yes.
→ → → →	
Attorney:	Well, the fact that Mr. Sampson may have been distracted at the time he fell may be helpful for our defense of this case. And we know that you are quite invested in mounting a strong defense to this case. We get the sense that you have a lot of pride in owning your business. And you should be proud. You've told us how you started your business from scratch, and how you might be at a point in the business where you start branching out.

Client:	Yes.
Attorney:	You love owning your business. The store means a lot to you. And, I imagine that to have someone—who is a regular customer at your store—claim that your actions caused him to fall and sustain all these injuries—well, I imagine it must feel quite hurtful.
Client:	Yes! I do feel hurt. Betrayed, almost. The store means the world to me. I have invested so much in it—time, energy, and my money. I can't let this lawsuit bring it and me down.
Attorney:	We can understand that. You are worried about the reputation of the store, your finances, and your livelihood.

* * *

C. Understand This! Here Are Some Take-Away Techniques from the Example

Here are a few techniques that you can identify from the last example:

1. *Take-Away Technique #1: The Attorney Followed the Client's Narrative*

We discussed in pillar three the importance of reflecting. We "reflected" on reflecting back to the clients the factual content of their stories. We "reflected" on reflecting back to the clients the values and emotions attached to their stories. Let's now "reflect" on how the attorney followed the client's narrative.

Clients seek legal representation because they have encountered some type of legal problem. This legal problem is often not isolated. There is a story—a narrative—that accompanies the problem. There is a plot that surrounds the problem. There are main and secondary characters that are involved in this problem. The characters' motives, beliefs, and actions likely have some influence on this problem.

Showing our clients that we can follow their narratives further helps to establish trust and rapport. It shows our clients that we acknowledge their stories. It shows our clients that we can still be active participants in helping them solve their legal problems, even though we are not characters actively involved in their stories.

Ms. James would likely be quite skeptical that her attorney could understand her story if part of the conversation would have played out in this ineffective way (the new part of the interview begins after the four arrows):

* * *

Attorney:	Hello, Ms. James. Thank you so much for coming by the office this morning. This is my paralegal, Stacy Garcia. I know you have spent some time speaking with Stacy over the telephone. She will be sitting in on the interview with me today and will help take notes of what is said during the interview.
Client:	Yes. Hello, Stacy.
Paralegal:	Hello, Ms. James.

Attorney:	So, Ms. James. Did you have any trouble finding our office?
Client:	Oh, no. It was easy.
Attorney:	Good. Well, Ms. James, we understand that you have received a letter that states that you are going to be sued in state court.
Client:	Yes. I received the letter a few days ago, and I have been worrying about it ever since. I have never been sued. I don't know what to do.

→   →   →   →

Attorney:	So you have some experience with lawsuits. You've done this before. So, you likely know how the process of this claim will go, and what to expect next.
Client:	Umm. No. I don't.

* * *

Or in this ineffective way:

* * *

Attorney:	Great. Well, why don't you tell us what has brought you in today, and how we might be able to help you?

Client:	Well, as the letter notes, I am the owner of *Dressing It Up!* It's a clothing store off of McGregor and Jewel. I started it all on my own. I do some of the designs, and I import some other designs. It has been really great owning my own store, and I have even considered opening up another branch of the store downtown. Well, that's until I received this lawsuit letter. Who knows what will happen now?
→ → → →	
Attorney:	Okay. So, you work at a clothing store. How long have you been an employee there? Could you give me the name of your boss? We likely will need to speak to him or her.

* * *

Or in this ineffective way:

* * *

Client:	Sure. It seems quite silly to me that he is threatening to sue me. You see. Mr. Sampson is somewhat of a regular customer. He gets all of his dress shirts and ties at my store. One day, I was assisting another customer when I saw him walk outside and fall. He took a few steps after exiting the store, and he slipped. Fell right on his backside.

Attorney:	Okay.
Client:	So, it had been raining most of the day. The sidewalk outside the store was a little damp. There were a few puddles. I remember I had told myself I needed to go put a warning sign outside the door—warning that the ground may be slippery. But, I got busy with another customer.
→ → → →	
Attorney:	So, you are not really familiar with Mr. Sampson. You have never really seen him before.
Client:	What? Umm. No. I just said that he is a regular customer.
Attorney:	Oh. Okay. I must have missed that. He is a regular customer. Okay. And you say that you really don't know what was happening at the time he fell because you were in another part of the store.
Client:	No. Not really. I saw him exit the store. I was busy with another customer. But, I saw him walk outside the store and fall down. I saw Mr. Sampson take a few steps outside the store, and fall on his backside.

* * *

In each of these above ineffective examples, the attorney did not show Ms. James that he was following her narrative. He did not show her that he was paying attention to her story. He did not solidify any trust or rapport that may have already been established. Rather, he likely made Ms. James feel like she was wasting his and her time. He likely made her feel like her words didn't matter. He likely made her feel like her narrative was one of those B or C movies that we forego watching in the middle of the night because we find some random infomercial more interesting.

Let's take a look at another pillar-four technique from the prior *effective* example.

2. Take-Away Technique #2: The Attorney Empathized with What the Client Is Going Through

Get ready. Take a breath. Here is another "touchy-feely" type of counseling technique that I hope you will use in your practice: empathy.

Showing our clients that we can empathize with what they are going through can help provide a really strong base to our conversation foundation. You may have heard that showing empathy—or being "empathic" or "empathetic"—is like trying to put yourself in someone else's shoes. Well, that is partially true. But, it may be somewhat difficult to understand. And, practically speaking, it may be really hard to achieve if you and your clients don't share the same shoe size.

When we empathize, we try to understand our clients' stories through their eyes. We try to understand what it must feel like to be experiencing what our clients are experiencing. We try to receive and process our clients' *unique* perspectives on their cases. And by the way, we don't need to feel sorry for our clients to try to understand their stories. Empathy is not sympathy. We can understand that our clients may feel quite troubled, desperate, or lost without necessarily feeling sorry for them.

Empathizing is more than just reflecting back to the clients whatever values or emotions the clients may have expressed to us. There is something more to empathy than simply saying something like "It must be very difficult for you." An empathic attorney will try to understand what the clients are going through that makes things difficult for them. An empathic attorney will try to understand why and how things are difficult for the clients. An empathic attorney will try to understand what might make things less difficult for the clients and why.

Let's revisit part of the Ms. James effective example. As you read the exchange, see if you can identify where the attorney demonstrates some empathy (the new part of the interview begins after the four arrows):

* * *

Attorney:	Well, the fact that Mr. Sampson may have been distracted at the time he fell may be helpful for our defense of this case. And we know that you are quite invested in mounting a strong defense to this case. We get the sense that you have a lot of pride in owning your business. And you should be proud. You've told us how you started your business from scratch, and how you might be at a point in the business where you start branching out.
Client:	Yes.

Attorney:	You love owning your business. The store means a lot to you. And, I imagine that to have someone—who is a regular customer at your store—claim that your actions caused him to fall and sustain all these injuries—well, I imagine it must feel quite hurtful.
Client:	Yes! I do feel hurt. Betrayed, almost. The store means the world to me. I have invested so much in it—time, energy, and my money. I can't let this lawsuit bring it and me down.
Attorney:	We can understand that. You are worried about the reputation of the store, your finances, and your livelihood.
→ → → →	
Client:	Yes.
Attorney:	I imagine this pending lawsuit is like a huge weight on your shoulders right now.
Client:	That is exactly how I feel. It's like I am carrying this burden on my shoulders, and I don't know how to lessen the weight.
Attorney:	Well, like we said earlier, the good thing is that you are here today seeking representation. We've worked on cases similar to your case. And, hopefully, we can help lessen or remove most of that weight—so that you can continue running your successful and fulfilling clothing store.

* * *

In this example, the attorney moved beyond simply identifying and reflecting back to Ms. James some of her values and emotions. The attorney empathized with her. He showed her that he not only was following her narrative, but *understanding it* as well. Here are three specific instances where the attorney demonstrated empathic responses:

- "And we know that you are quite invested in mounting a strong defense to this case. We get the sense that you have a lot of pride in owning your business. And you should be proud. You've told us how you started your business from scratch, and how you might be at a point in the business where you start branching out."

- "You love owning your business. The store means a lot to you. And, I imagine that to have someone—who is a regular customer at your store—claim that your actions caused him to fall and sustain all these injuries—well, I imagine it must feel quite hurtful."

- "I imagine this pending lawsuit is like a huge weight on your shoulders right now."

Notice that in each of the instances the attorney showed Ms. James that he understood what she was going through. He showed her that he understood how this potential lawsuit was impacting her daily life. He showed her that he was gaining a better picture of Ms. James. Who is she? What makes her tick? What is important to her? And why are these things important to her?

a.   Additional Tip #1: Use of "I Imagine" and "It Must Be Like"

Notice also how the attorney used the phrase "I imagine" to signal to Ms. James that he was trying to fill in some of the gaps of her story with *his understanding of her perspective*. Phrases like "I imagine" or "It must be like" are helpful ways to start some of your empathic responses. They let your clients know that you are trying to think and feel like they think and feel.

b.   Additional Tip #2: Pay Attention to the Client's Confirmation of Your Empathic Responses

Notice also how Ms. James confirmed whether the attorney's gap-filling attempts were successful. There were several points in the conversation where she said "yes" or "exactly." We strengthen our professional relationships with our clients when we are able to correctly empathize and reflect back to the clients what they are going through. It strengthens the already established trust and rapport. The clients begin to think, "Yes. This attorney gets it." This helps the clients to further open up and participate in the professional relationship.

Don't worry if you don't always get it, though. As Ms. James did in some of the earlier *ineffective* narrative examples, your clients will correct you if you are not getting the right complete picture. They will hit "pause" on the remote and replay what they said. But, they may only willingly replay a few times. You only get a few chances to build that trust and rapport. If you don't show your clients that you are actively listening and trying to understand their stories, they will stop telling their stories. Like your satellite dish in a rough storm, they will shut down. That trust and rapport will be deleted.

CHAPTER 11

The Fifth and Final Pillar—Take Time to Explain to the Clients, in Layman's Terms, How the Law Applies to Their Problems

The fifth and final pillar to the conversation foundation is explaining to the clients, in layman's terms, how the law applies to their problems. Let me try to explain this pillar in layman's terms.

A. Speak My Language, Please!

So, I started off this book by talking about how attorneys are problems solvers. Clients typically seek legal representation because they are faced with some problem—some legal situation that requires assistance. We have spent some time focusing on building trust and rapport with our clients so that they open up and tell us their stories. We have spent some time talking about techniques that can show that we are actively listening and reflecting back to our clients the content, values, and emotions relating to their stories. We have spent some time trying to understand what it must feel like for our clients to be facing their problems. Now, let's focus on talking to our clients about how the law applies to their problems. Yes! We can now impress our clients with all of our fancy legal analysis! But, let's also try to impress our clients by speaking their language.

Yes. We should try to speak our clients' language when we explain to them how the law applies to their problems. Now, I'm not asking that you take a quick *Rosetta Stone* learn-a-different-language course. I mean that we should try to speak to our clients at a level that they will understand.

1. *Consider Outlining, in Layman's Terms, How the Client Interview Will Proceed*

Subpart 2 below will "explain" how we should explain the law to our clients in a manner that they can understand. This explanation includes the law itself, and how the law applies to our clients' legal problems. Before we get to Subpart 2, let's talk about another portion of the client interview where speaking our clients' language would be beneficial: during a roadmap or outline of the client interview.

Let's revisit part of the beginning of the Ms. James slip and fall example and see how the attorney speaks at Ms. James' level. Prepare yourselves. This example is a lengthy exchange between the attorney and Ms. James. You will see that I added a roadmap of the interview and some discussion of some "administrative items" to the start of the client interview. Chapters 13 and 14 of the book will examine the benefits of including a roadmap in an initial client interview, as well as highlight some of the "administrative items" that we should discuss with our clients during the interview.

As you read this exchange, see if the attorney spoke to Ms. James at a level that she could understand. See if the attorney provided Ms. James with an easy outline of the initial consultation. And see if the attorney summarized some of the "administrative items" that attorneys are professionally obligated to speak to their clients about. Here is the exchange (the new part of the interview begins after the four arrows):

* * *

Attorney: Wonderful. Well, we understand that you are worried about this letter that you received that threatens a lawsuit against you. We'd love to spend some time just letting you tell us a little more about what may have happened that might have led to this potential lawsuit. And as you tell us your story, Ms. James, we'd love for you to be as open and honest as possible. Because the more information that we know about your situation, the better we are able to assist you.

Client: Yes. Okay.

→ → → →

Attorney: But, before we hand over the stage to you, we'd just like to spend a few minutes outlining how the rest of this initial meeting will go—just so that you have a better idea as to what to expect during today's interview.

Client:	Okay.
Attorney:	So, we will start by spending a little time discussing some items that were included in the paperwork that we forwarded to you. As lawyers, we are bound by something called the rules of professional responsibility. And what this means is that we must act ethically when we represent you and all our other clients.
Client:	Yes. I remember reading the paperwork.
Attorney:	Good. So, you might remember reading some information on things like confidentiality, conflicts of interest, and billing.
Client:	Yes. I do.
Attorney:	Good. So we will spend a few minutes talking about some of these items. Then, we will hand the floor to you, and let you tell us what has brought you here today. We like to call this part of the interview *your* opportunity to tell us *your* story.
Client:	Okay.
Attorney:	So, after we have had an opportunity to listen to your story, we might ask some clarifying questions to help us better understand what may be going on. And we might summarize some of the information that you have told us, just to make sure that we are getting a good and accurate picture of your story.
Client:	Okay.

Attorney:	After that, we might discuss some initial legal issues that we have been able to identify so far. And then, all together, we might begin to discuss some initial possible solutions to your legal situation—some legal and non-legal options that we may want to further explore during the course of the representation.
Client:	I see.
Attorney:	By then, our scheduled time for our initial consultation may be coming to a close. So, we will try to conclude the interview by providing a quick summary of the main points of the interview, as well as talking about any further steps that we may plan to pursue in the next few weeks.
Client:	Okay.
Attorney:	All right. Well, are there any questions so far on what to expect during the rest of the interview?
Client:	No. I think I'm good.
Attorney:	Great. Well, let us just take a few minutes now to talk about some items like confidentiality, billing, and conflicts of interest. I understand that you and Stacy have already discussed some of these items.
Client:	Yes. We did.
Attorney:	Okay. So, we have been hired by your insurance company to represent you in this

	case. Basically, that just means that we are *your* attorneys. We can't go and represent Mr. Sampson, for example.
Client:	Okay.
Attorney:	And, the insurance company will be paying us to defend you in this case. That is one of the good reasons for having insurance. And my hourly rate and the hourly rates for Stacy and some of my associate attorneys were outlined in the letter that Stacy sent to you.
Client:	Yes.
Attorney:	As the letter also noted, confidentiality is very important to the attorney-client relationship. What this means is that, generally, what you say to us will be kept in confidence—it will be kept within the walls of this law firm. For instance, we can't go and tell Mr. Sampson any of the information that you discuss with us unless you've authorized us to disclose this information. As the letter also noted, there are some exceptions to confidentiality. But, we don't anticipate any of them being an issue in this case. Of course, if they do become an issue, we will definitely let you know. Are there any questions thus far as to confidentiality?
Client:	No. Not at this time.
Attorney:	Great. Well, finally, I know that Stacy also spoke to you about conflicts of interest. She

	may have asked you for some of the names of the parties associated with this case, and perhaps their contact information.
Client:	Yes. I remember that.
Attorney:	Well, as attorneys, we can't represent clients whose interests conflict with, or are adverse to, any of our current clients or former clients. So, what we do is run the names that you provided to us, and the names that we discover in the case file, against a client database in our office to see if there are any conflicts. And so far, everything looks good.
Client:	Great.
Attorney:	Okay. Well, are there any questions that you may have at this time?
Client:	No. I don't think so.
Attorney:	Wonderful. Well, we are now at the point of the interview where we hand over the stage to you and you get to tell us your story. So, why don't you tell us what has brought you here today and how we might be able to help you?

* * *

In the above example, the attorney spoke to Ms. James in a manner that Ms. James could understand. First, notice how the attorney took some time to provide a short and understandable outline of the client interview. As Chapter 14 will describe, the roadmap of the client interview provides our clients with an understanding of what the client interview will look like. It highlights the route that the attorney and client will take during the interview. The attorney in the Ms. James example spoke Ms. James' language as he outlined the route to her. He spoke at her level without belittling Ms. James or sounding demeaning.

Second, notice how the attorney explained to Ms. James some of the "administrative" matters that attorneys are obligated to speak to their clients about. But, instead of explaining these concepts with legalese or reading the professional rules verbatim, the attorney tried to paraphrase the concepts and explain them in a manner that could hopefully be understood by Ms. James. Imagine if the attorney had started reading the rule on confidentiality and then listed the various exceptions to confidentiality. Now, imagine if the attorney also read how the rule on confidentiality differs from privilege. These concepts can be difficult for some attorneys to understand. So, it could potentially get quite confusing for the client. Had the attorney spoken to Ms. James at such a high lawyerly level, she may have started to feel like she is inferior, dumb, or so out of place in the law firm office that she would want to hide under the conference room table.

2. *Explain the Law and How the Law Applies to the Client's Problem in a Manner That the Client Will Understand*

In Subpart 1, the attorney explained, in layman's terms, some "administrative" items, like confidentiality, billing, and conflicts of interest. The attorney also outlined a roadmap for the client interview in a manner that Ms. James could understand.

Now, let's take another look at a portion of the Ms. James example to see how the attorney could begin to explain and apply some of the relevant premises liability law to the facts that Ms. James presented in the interview. Yes! We are at that point where the attorney can impress the client with all of his wonderful legal analysis! Warning: This example is also a little long. There is some explanation of the law going on. And there is some application of the law to the facts of the case going on. So, take a breath. As you read the exchange, see if the attorney explains and applies the law in layman's terms (the new part of the interview begins after the four arrows):

* * *

Attorney:	We can understand that. You are worried about the reputation of the store, your finances, and your livelihood.
Client:	Yes.
Attorney:	I imagine this pending lawsuit is like a huge weight on your shoulders right now.
Client:	That is exactly how I feel. It's like I am carrying this burden on my shoulders, and I don't know how to lessen the weight.
Attorney:	Well, like we said earlier, the good thing is that you are here today seeking representation. We've worked on cases similar to your case. And, hopefully, we can help lessen or remove most of that weight—so that you can continue running your successful and fulfilling clothing store.

→   →   →   →

Client:	That is good to hear.
Attorney:	So, it sounds like your case is the typical premises liability case. Or, as some people sometimes say— your typical slip and fall case. And like I said, our firm has handled many slip and fall cases.
Client:	Okay. Well, that's great.
Attorney:	In these types of cases, a business—much like your clothing store—is sued for injuries allegedly sustained as a result of the business owner's negligence or the negligence of, say, one of the employees who works at the business.
Client:	Okay.
Attorney:	What that means is that the person who claims that he was injured is saying that the business did something wrong—that it did not act with proper care. And that this lack of proper care lead to the person's injuries.
Client:	So, I guess the fact that I didn't put out the warning sign is my lack of care?
Attorney:	Well, at this point, it appears like that is where Mr. Sampson will likely go with his case. You see, in these premises liability cases, there can be some liability placed on the business—meaning the business may be found at fault for the accident—if the business owner or some employee was aware of some potential problem at the business, and did not fix it or warn about it.

Client:	Okay.
Attorney:	So, you mentioned that you knew that it had been raining earlier on the day that Mr. Sampson fell. You also mentioned that you wanted to put out a warning sign outside the store to warn folks that the sidewalk might be slippery. But, you weren't able to do so, because you got busy with another client.
Client:	Right.
Attorney:	So, I imagine that Mr. Sampson will likely argue that you were aware of the slippery sidewalk, but you did not act with proper care to fix or warn about the slippery sidewalk.
Client:	I see. So, I guess I'll likely be found at fault for his slip and fall?
Attorney:	Well, it's not necessarily a slam-dunk for Mr. Sampson. He still could face some challenges in his case.
Client:	Really? How?
Attorney:	Well, you mentioned that he might have been preoccupied with his cell phone at the time that he was exiting your store. Assuming that there is some fault on the store—which he still would have to first establish—his preoccupation with his phone could limit the amount of money that he could recover from this accident, or it could eliminate it entirely.
Client:	Really?

Attorney:	Well, yes. That is a possibility. But, we are just at the initial stages of this case. We still have more facts to gather. And we will likely want to speak to some of the other customers who were present on the day that Mr. Sampson fell—to help build support for your version of the events.
Client:	Sure. I understand.
Attorney:	But, in our state, there is something called comparative negligence. In premises liability cases, in addition to the court examining whether the business owner may have been at fault for causing an accident, the court will also examine the fault for the person who fell. And if the person who fell is, say, 30% at fault for causing his own fall, then his recovery is reduced by 30%.
Client:	Interesting.
Attorney:	Yes. And if the person who fell is more than 50% at fault for causing his fall, then he is barred from recovering anything for his fall.
Client:	Okay. I think I get it.
Attorney:	So, based on the facts that we know so far, I imagine we will likely want to establish that Mr. Sampson was so preoccupied with his phone that he was not able to see the puddles outside. If he had been walking about earlier in the day, he should have been aware that it had

	been raining. Most folks expect that there will be some water on the sidewalk after it rains. So, he should have known that the sidewalk could be wet and slippery. And he should have taken better precaution—instead of walking outside the store with eyes fixated on his cell phone.
Client:	Okay.
Attorney:	I know that this may seem like a lot of information at this point. Do you have any questions so far?
Client:	No. Not at this time. I think things are making pretty good sense so far.

* * *

In this effective example, the attorney did not try to impress Ms. James with super fancy thesaurus-type words. He did not provide some extensive summary of the law in a manner that would be better suited for a scholarly law journal. He simply was able to explain some premises liability law in a manner that Ms. James could understand. He also provided some initial legal analysis at a level that Ms. James could follow.

Let's take a look at some specific pillar-five techniques below in Subpart B.

B. Apply and Explain Away! Here Are Some Take-Away Techniques from the Examples

Here are a few techniques from the two effective examples presented in this chapter:

1. *Take-Away Technique #1: The Attorney Did Not Rush the Explanation or Application of the Law*

Notice how the attorney took some time to explain the law. In the first example, the attorney slowly explained some of the "administrative" matters to Ms. James—the billing arrangement, what confidentiality means, and what a conflict of interest is.

In the second example, the attorney took some time to explain the law of premises liability, and how this law applied to the facts that Ms. James had presented in the interview.

In both examples, the attorney did not feel compelled to condense everything into one or two sentences. The attorney also did not provide some exhaustive and confusing report on whether or not Ms. James would be found liable for Mr. Sampson's injuries. The attorney understood that Ms. James needed more information than simply one or two sentences. And he understood that she needed this information presented in a simple manner. So, he did not rush the explanation or application of the law. And he provided a more detailed, yet easy-to-follow, summary of his initial legal analysis.

Most of our clients will not have their JDs. They will not understand what "Black Letter Law" is. They won't know what elements or factors are. They may not know what a "legal issue" is. Remember back to your first few weeks of law school. Sorry, there I go again—rehashing potentially negative memories. But, remember how long it took you to gain an understanding of what it meant to think like a lawyer. Remember that it took some time to realize what a legally significant fact was. Remember that it likely took you some time to get the idea of what legal application is all about. I-RAC, C-RAC, or CREAC? There was a lot to digest. And you likely did not take it all in during a single sitting. So, don't stuff the law and application down your clients' throats. It took you some time to understand what explanation and application of the law is all about. Give your clients some time as well.

2. *Take-Away Technique #2: The Attorney Spoke in Plain English*

Notice also how the attorney spoke in plain English. The attorney did not feel compelled to use fancy words when he explained the law to Ms. James or how the law applied to the facts that Ms. James had presented in the interview. If he did use some potentially fancy words—like comparative negligence—he took some time to explain them to Ms. James in layman's terms.

Don't feel compelled to impress your clients with words that you remember from your SAT prep. You don't have to have a thesaurus next to you to ensure that you are utilizing the lengthiest and most eloquent-sounding words that are conceivably imaginable and that articulate the distinct and momentous revelations that you want your clients to comprehend. Don't do it. Your clients will need a thesaurus just to try to understand you. Just speak plainly. Use simple words. Your clients will like it.

3. *Take-Away Technique #3: The Attorney Did Not Guarantee Any Specific Results*

Notice also that the attorney was careful in how he explained the legal application. He did not guarantee any results. He cautioned Ms. James that they were just in the initial fact-gathering stage of the case, and that there was still more information that was needed to fully evaluate her case.

If our clients are coming to see us because they have a legal problem, they will pounce on any reference to a potential satisfactory answer to this problem. And we really can't blame them. They likely were dealing with this problem long before we got involved. They may have had some sleepless nights because of their problems. Or, at the very least, their problems have been a bit of a "problem" for each of them. So, we need to be careful when we shine some light at the end of their tunnels. Watch your words when you apply the law to the facts of your clients' cases. Words and phrases like "often," "at this point," "perhaps," and "may" *may* help you. Leave yourself some wiggle room. Be careful to not guarantee results you can't produce.

Now, let's wiggle on down to Part 4 of the book for a detailed description of the specific parts to a client interview.

Descriptions and Illustrations for a Client Interview—Let's Break It Down

Now that we have spent some time discussing the five pillars to the conversation foundation, let's spend some time breaking down a basic client interview. You will see that there is some overlap in the information presented to you in this Part with the information that was presented in Part 3 of the book.

Part 3 covered the foundation to a conversation with a client and included an extended exchange with Ms. Loretta James regarding a potential premises liability lawsuit against her.

Part 4 of the book uses the conversation foundation to provide an outline for the basic parts to a client interview. And by basic, I mean basic. You will find that this outline is not the only way to conduct a client interview. For example, the amount of time we ultimately spend on each part of the interview and the order of each part may vary. They may vary depending on the extent of information that we have available relating to our clients' cases prior to the interviews. They may vary depending on the level of experience our clients have with working with attorneys. And they may vary depending on *our level* of experience with client interviews. As our experience with client interviews increases, we will learn to be more flexible in the way we conduct our interviews. Like athletes who train for a sport, we learn what works for us. And we learn what we still need to work on.

So, Chapters 12-17 provide an outline for the basic parts to a client interview. You'll likely remember some of the parts of the interview from the Ms. James premises liability hypothetical. If you can't or don't want to remember, the chapters also provide some additional hypothetical exchanges between an attorney and a client to demonstrate some of the parts to the client interview. As I mentioned, the outline may not apply to every case that you will encounter. But if the five pillars were the foundation to a conversation with our clients, consider the outline as a simple blueprint to the conversation. Consider each part of the outline as a room that you want to create during the conversation. Design choices are left to you. Let's start creating!

CHAPTER 12

Before the Interview: Dealing with "Administrative Items"

So, many of you may be wondering why I even have this "dealing with administrative items" chapter in the outline for a client interview, when the chapter title also says that it occurs *before* the interview. Well, first of all, good active reading! Kudos to you! You have been really paying attention to my chapter and subchapter titles! I'm sure your active listening skills will be just as great!

Secondly, as attorneys, we have an ethical code that guides our legal profession. We can't just get by like the character *Saul Goodman* from the television shows *Breaking Bad* and *Better Call Saul* (great shows, by the way!).

Unless we want to risk getting disbarred or facing some public shaming in one of our state bar journals, we should try to follow our Rules for Professional Conduct. Some of these rules require that our clients be made aware of certain matters that impact the attorney-client relationship. Our clients need to be aware of matters like confidentiality, potential conflicts of interest, and any billing or fee arrangements associated with our possible representation of them.

Now many of us have client intake forms that describe and help lessen the amount of time that we spend on what I call "administrative" or "housekeeping" matters. We may require our clients to fill out these forms before we have the client interview. We may have our paralegals or secretaries follow up with our clients to confirm that they have received and completed these forms. Nevertheless, it is always important to make sure that our clients understand these matters and any other office policies that may be related to our potential representation of them.

You may remember that the attorney discussed with Ms. James some of these "administrative" matters in the premises liability example in Chapter 11. As you will see in Chapter 14 below, we can cover some of these initial matters in the initial client interview—right after we greet our clients and provide a roadmap for how the interview will proceed. As you will also see in Chapter 14, our clients' education and familiarity with the attorney-client relationship will impact how much time we spend discussing these "administrative" matters with our clients.

CHAPTER 13

Show Your Manners! You Don't Have to Be Best Friends to Still Greet and Welcome the Client

We have all heard the saying, "You only have one chance to make a good first impression." Now, it is not like you are competing for the "first impression rose" on the television shows *The Bachelor* or *The Bachelorette*. But, we do want our initial meetings with our clients to set a good tone for the rest of the season—I mean, for the rest of the interview.

If we have never met with a specific client before, the first few minutes of the client interview may be particularly significant to establishing a strong professional relationship. Remember the first pillar to the conversation foundation? We want to let our clients know that we are there to help them. A friendly greeting and some short small talk can help show our clients that we won't bite. Seating your clients in a position that limits the power dynamic of "big, smart attorneys" and "little, weak clients" can also help create a more welcoming environment to your clients.

A. Seat Your Clients to Limit Any Power Dynamic

As you plan out your client interviews, consider where you want your clients to sit. Consider any physical barriers, like a conference room table or desk, that might create distance between you and your clients. These barriers create an obvious physical distance between you and your clients, since you are literally further away in space from your clients. But, more importantly, these barriers can also create a situation where your clients feel less connected to you—an emotional distance, if you will.

The seating arrangement during the client interviews might make your clients feel more intimidated and less likely to want to open up and participate in the attorney-client relationship. So, try to reduce the physical barriers between you and your clients whenever possible. A circular table may help. If you only have square or rectangular tables, consider seating your clients in a position where they are not directly across from you. Try to seat your clients in area that is more at an angle towards you, rather than directly across from you. The following graphics may help further explain this concept:

Client

Attorney

2nd Attorney or
Office Paralegal

Client

Attorney

2nd Attorney or
Office Paralegal

B. Greet Your Clients with Some Initial, Uncontroversial Chitchat

In addition to considering where you want your clients to sit during the client interview, consider also starting your interview with a friendly greeting and some simple small talk. A simple "hello" and some initial back and forth chatting on some uncontroversial topic can show our clients that the interview is not the equivalent of a child's visit to the dentist. A warm welcome and some chitchat can place some anxious clients at ease.

Let's take a look at a short example. As you read the exchange, see what uncontroversial topic the attorney uses to help welcome the client:

* * *

Attorney:	Hello, Mr. Smith. It is a pleasure to meet you. My name is Stephanie Williams.
Client:	Hello, Ms. Williams.
Attorney:	Thank you for taking the time to come speak with us today. Please. Have a seat right here.
Client:	Thank you.
Attorney:	Here with us today is my paralegal, Brian Chang. I believe you have already had a chance to speak with Brian over the phone. Brian will be sitting in on the interview with me today and will be taking notes on what is said during the interview.
Client:	Yes. Hello, Brian.

Paralegal:	Hello, Mr. Smith.
Attorney:	So, Mr. Smith, did you have any problems finding our office?
Client:	Oh, no. Your secretary was able to give me some good directions. And, I was able to pull up the map on my phone.
Attorney:	Yes. Isn't it pretty incredible how much technology we have on our phones? I see my five year-old playing a game on my phone, and I try to explain to him that I did not have these types of games when I was little.
Client:	Yes. It is pretty amazing how much they can put inside such small phones.
Attorney:	That's so true.
Client:	(Nodding head "yes").
Attorney:	Well, Mr. Smith, we understand that you are here today to speak to us about a situation with your employer.

* * *

In the above example, the attorney used some simple small talk about directions and technology on cell phones as a bit of an icebreaker. The attorney did not feel compelled to jump right into the client interview. Rather, she used small talk to help get the client more relaxed and settled into the interview. She showed the client that the interview is much like a conversation. She didn't pressure the client with some initial difficult question. She simply asked whether the client had any difficulty finding the office, and the client responded by bringing up cell phone technology. What followed was a nice, brief exchange about cell phone maps and games that helped welcome the client.

Another icebreaker topic that may seem cliché, but is nonetheless effective at helping welcome your clients is a question or statement about the weather. Unless our clients have been in an underground bunker for an extended period of time—like the *Netflix* television show character *Kimmy Schmidt*—they typically don't have to prepare to answer a question about the weather. Most clients will be able to chitchat briefly about how sunny, cold, or rainy it has been lately. So, provide your clients with a friendly greeting and hit up the small talk! It will help settle your clients. And a more settled client is a more willing participant in the attorney-client relationship.

CHAPTER 14

Roadmap! Let the Clients Know Where You Are Going with the Interview

A. An Ode to Paper Maps—Yes, Paper Maps!

Some of you may not know this. But, some of us had to purchase maps at the local convenience store before we would go on a trip or vacation. Yes. Pay—for a map. The maps were pieces of paper that had pictures. Yes. They were paper. They showed streets, rest stops, and parks. And, if you were lucky, the map had a nice little graph that showed how many miles it would take for you to get to your destination.

Before a trip, many of us would either highlight our route on the map, or we'd write down the list of streets and stops that we were planning to take on our trip. We would provide a roadmap for our trip with a physical map.

Well, many of us have ditched our paper maps along with our station wagons. We now have *GPS*. And our phones, tablets, or vehicles can show us our maps and literally tell us where to go.

Yes. They can get quite snarky as they vocalize their "rerouting" when we don't exactly follow their suggested routes. But the good thing is we don't have to look at a piece of paper to roadmap our trip. We can still preview what our trip will look like without flipping through those pages. And who ever figured out how to refold those maps the correct way, anyway?

B. Mapping the Client Interview

Just as we like to preview the streets and stops of an upcoming trip, our clients like a preview of what the client interview will look like. Client interviews may seem quite intimidating for some clients. Unless we are dealing with clients who have experience working with attorneys, many of our clients will enter our offices for a client interview wishing there was some *CliffsNotes* version of what to expect during the interview. So, it is helpful to provide a short roadmap to our clients of what the client interview will look like.

You may remember the roadmap the attorney provided to Ms. James in Chapter 11 of the book. Here's another example of a roadmap for an initial client interview. As you read the exchange, see if the attorney successfully provides a short preview of what the interview will look like:

* * *

Attorney:	Mr. Sawyer, we are going to spend some time learning a little more about your situation. But, before we fully get into that, we would like to spend just a few minutes outlining what today's initial interview will look like—just so

	that you have a better understanding of what to expect today.
Client:	Okay.
Attorney:	So, we will start by spending a little time discussing some items that were in the paperwork that we forwarded to you. As lawyers, we are bound by something called the rules of professional responsibility. And what this means is that we must act ethically when we represent you and all our other clients.
Client:	Yes. I remember reading the paperwork.
Attorney:	Good. So, you might remember reading some information on things like confidentiality, conflicts of interest, and billing.
Client:	Yes. I do.
Attorney:	Good. So we will spend a few minutes talking about some of these items. Then, we will hand the floor to you, and let you tell us what has brought you here today. We want to learn more about your legal matter. We want to understand your thoughts and concerns about your legal matter, and how we might be able to help you. We like to call this your opportunity to tell us your story.
Client:	Okay.
Attorney:	So, after we have had an opportunity to listen to your story, we might ask some clarifying questions to help us better understand what

	may be going on. And we might summarize some of the information that you have told us, just to make sure that we are getting a good and accurate picture of your story.
Client:	Okay.
Attorney:	After that, we might discuss some initial legal issues that we have been able to identify so far. And then, all together, we might begin to discuss some initial possible solutions to your problem—some legal and non-legal options that we may want to further explore during the course of the representation.
Client:	I see.
Attorney:	By then, our scheduled time for our initial consultation may be coming to a close. So, we will try to conclude the interview by providing a quick summary of the main points of the interview. We will also talk about any further steps that we plan to pursue in the next few weeks.
Client:	Okay.
Attorney:	All right. Well, are there any questions so far on what to expect during today's interview?
Client:	No. I think I'm good.
Attorney:	Great. Well, let's take a few minutes and talk about some items like confidentiality, billing, and conflicts of interest.

* * *

In the above example, the attorney spent a few minutes out of the initial consultation to provide a roadmap to the client of the client interview. Here are two potential benefits for providing a roadmap of the client interview:

1. *The Roadmap Provides a Highlighted Path of the Client Interview for New or Inexperienced Clients*

Providing a roadmap to our clients allows them to have a better understanding of what to expect during the interview. It acts like a description of an entrée in a restaurant menu. It gives the clients a glimpse of what they will taste later.

And like reading a menu at a restaurant that we frequently visit, we likely do not need to be as detailed with our roadmaps if our clients are repeat or experienced clients, or if they are some kind of general counsel for some company. These types of clients are already familiar with the attorney-client relationship. They likely have been through a few initial client interviews. They've "been there." And they've "done that" already.

So, we can modify how detailed we get with our roadmaps based on who our clients are and the level of experience they may have with attorneys. The same rings true with our descriptions of some of our ethical items, like confidentiality, billing, and conflicts of interest. We don't have to be as specific with some of our descriptions about our ethical obligations with say, a general counsel, as we would with other clients. As I mentioned in Chapter 11, the speed and level of sophistication to which we speak with our clients will vary based on how educated our clients are and how familiar they are with the attorney-client relationship.

2. *The Roadmap Provides an Outline of What to Cover During the Interview for New or Inexperienced Attorneys*

Although the primary purpose for providing a roadmap of the interview to our clients is to give the clients a better understanding of where the interview will go, the roadmap has one particular striking benefit for attorneys—it helps keep us on track!

Yes. The roadmap sets out for our clients a highlighted path for what they can expect during the interview. But, it also provides a highlighted path *for us* of an outline of what to discuss with our clients.

Remember our outlines for our law school oral arguments? Remember how those outlines helped provide us with something to say during our oral arguments if we stumbled or got nervous? Well, a roadmap for a client interview can act as an outline for what we should cover during the interview if we similarly stumble or get nervous.

We all learn to be more flexible in the way we conduct our interviews as our experience and comfort with client interviews increases. We learn to put "our stamp" on our client interviews. We learn to make them "our own" client interviews. Until you are able to take ownership of your client interviews, or until you are able to find that unique stamp and ink, you can use your interview roadmap as a checklist for what to cover during your client interviews. I bet the roadmap checklist will still come in handy even after you find your special stamp and ink!

CHAPTER 15

Let's Go on a Fact-Gathering Hunt: Listening to and Understanding the Client's Story

After we have provided our clients with a roadmap of the interview, we move into the heart of the client interview. We begin to really work with pillars two, three, and four of the conversation foundation. We want to let our clients talk. And we want to listen to and try to understand their stories. We want to go on a fact-gathering hunt.

As we embark on our fact-gathering hunt, we should try to limit close-ended questions at first, so that our clients have more freedom to describe their problems *as they see* their problems. If we immediately jump into specific factual questions that we feel are most relevant to the legal issues in play—without fully hearing the clients' stories—we may miss a lot of significant information from the clients. Our clients may neglect to tell us facts that are highly relevant to their cases. They may not trust us enough at this point to disclose potentially embarrassing or negative facts. Or, they may feel like certain facts are not important, since we did not *specifically ask* questions relating to these facts right at the start.

So, yes, we may limit what we are able to discover in our client interviews when we start off with close-ended questions. Starting our client interviews with "yes" or "no" questions, or questions that our clients believe only require a one or two word answer, may harm or spoil our fact-gathering hunt. It is like reading the last few pages of a book before you read anything else. We may get to know the ending of our clients' stories, but we will know little about how and why the stories happened. We will not know who our clients are, what they value, and how we might be able to help them solve their legal problems. Our fact-gathering hunt may lead us down an unproductive rabbit trail.

You may remember the fact-gathering portion of the Ms. James slip and fall example from Chapter 8 of the book. Let's take a look at another example of how to start the fact-gathering portion of a client interview. As you read the exchange, notice how the attorney tries to encourage the client to be open and honest:

* * *

Attorney:	So, Ms. De Luca, now that we have talked a little about how the interview will proceed today, we would really like to take some time to listen to you. We'd like to listen to your story.
Client:	Okay.

> Attorney: And while you are telling us your story, Ms. De Luca, we'd like it if you could tell us anything and everything that might be related to why you have sought legal representation. Because the more information we have from you, the better equipped we are to help serve you.
>
> Client: Okay. Yes.
>
> Attorney: Great. So, what has brought you here today? And how might we be able to help you?

* * *

The attorney in the above example started the fact-gathering phase of the interview with a few broad, open-ended questions. Saying something like "What has brought you here today?" or "How might we be able to help you?" are simple ways to start the fact-gathering hunt. These types of questions gently move the microphone to the clients. They let the clients take over the center stage without flustering them with a possible spotlight directly on top of them. Ease that bright light. Dim it. The start of the client interview is not a sprint. We don't need every single piece of information from our clients within the first fifteen minutes of the interview.

We also don't need to continuously interrupt our clients while they tell us their stories. As our clients speak, we can take notes of any names, dates, and locations that might require clarification. We can seek to clarify this information when we switch from open-ended questions that help clients tell their general narratives to more close-ended questions that might help us fill in some of the details of their narratives.

A. Identifying and Understanding the Relevant Facts

Part of our work as problem solvers involves identifying and understanding the relevant facts to our clients' stories. So, as we listen to our clients tell us their stories, we should pay attention to specific facts that may impact how we evaluate their cases. We can think of ourselves as journalists wanting to break an important story. We want answers to the "Who," "What," "When," "Where," "Why," and "How" of our clients' stories.

1. *Working with Clients Who Freely Tell Their Stories*

Some of our clients will freely answer some of the "Who," "What," "When," "Where," "Why," and "How" questions as they discuss their stories. One or two open-ended questions may open the gates to a flood of legally significant information. When this happens, we should be ready to take sufficient notes of what the clients are saying. We should thank our clients for sharing so much information, and we should follow-up with any specific close-ended questions that may help clarify some of the information that the clients provided. Finally, we should take the time to summarize some of the factual information back to the clients. This reflection back to the clients of the *factual content* of the clients' stories shows our clients that we have been paying attention to the details of their stories. It lets our clients know that we are beginning to identify facts that might impact our legal analysis.

You may remember that the attorney in the Ms. James slip and fall example summarized some of the factual content that Ms. James provided in the interview. Let's take a look at how the attorney in the following example begins to summarize the factual content of the client's story. As you read the exchange, notice how the attorney first explains why he may have been taking some notes during the client's storytelling. Notice also how the attorney encourages the client to correct any factual information that he may have misunderstood or mischaracterized. Here's the example:

* * *

Attorney:	Thank you for sharing that, Mr. O'Brien. That was very helpful.
Client:	Sure.
Attorney:	So, you may have seen us taking some notes while you were telling us the information from your story. Now, we weren't doodling or writing down our grocery list. We were jotting down some of the information that you were telling us—so that we can make sure that we have the most accurate information possible relating to your story.
Client:	Yes. I understand.
Attorney:	So, since we do want to make sure that we have the most accurate information possible relating to your story, we'd like to just spend a few minutes summarizing some of the information back to you. Again, we are just trying to make sure that we understand the facts *as you have told them to us*. So, if at any time, you notice that we said something incorrectly or if we misrepresented what you

	just told us, please stop us and correct us. We won't be upset about it at all. In fact, we would greatly appreciate it. It just helps us get a better picture of what is going on with your story.
Client:	Sure. Okay.
Attorney:	Great. So, Mr. O'Brien, you are here because you were injured while working at a drilling site. And you want to discuss possible options in filing a claim against your employer.
Client:	Yes.

* * *

2. *Working with Clients Who Don't Freely Tell Their Stories*

I mentioned that we might get a flood of information from our clients with one or two open-ended questions. Our clients may have been so frustrated with their legal problems that they may be bursting at the seams to tell their stories. They may be ready, willing, and more than able to state their version of the events.

However, we may not always be fortunate to get such a flood of information from our clients as a result of just a few questions. There may be roadblocks in place that stifle the exchange of information. When we encounter some of these roadblocks, we may want to pull some close-ended questions out of our back pockets. We can try to *gently prompt* our clients with direct questions that help focus them on particular parts of their stories that require further clarification. Close-ended questions can be helpful in client interviews—if they are asked at the right time. They often help us connect the dots of our clients' stories when the clients don't initially connect them for us.

B. Identifying and Understanding the Clients' Values and Emotions

As Chapters 9 and 10 emphasized, in addition to understanding the factual content of our clients' stories, we also need to pay attention to the values and emotions associated with our clients' stories. We should try to find out how our clients feel about their legal problems. We should try to understand what our clients' goals are with respect to their legal problems. We should try to empathize with our clients as they experience their legal problems.

As we actively listen to our clients' stories, we begin to better understand our clients. We may not fit into our clients' shoes. But, we may be able to walk in their shoes. We may begin to understand what our clients' legal problems are really about. We may begin to understand what motivates our clients. We may begin to understand what they value.

Just as we should reflect the factual content of our clients' stories, we should also reflect back to our clients the values and emotions that are associated with their stories. This reflection lets our clients know that we have not only followed them through the fact-gathering hunt, but that we have also understood the narrative that these facts create. Understanding our clients' facts and narratives will help pave the way for a more effective legal analysis. Chapters 23 and 24 will provide you more information on empathy and how the use of reflection can be an effective tool in the client interview.

CHAPTER 16

Trying to Solve That Word Problem: Using Legal Analysis to Help Solve the Client's Problem

After the clients have told us their stories, and after we have had an opportunity to show our clients that we understand their stories, we should try to spend some time using that legal analysis that we learned so well in law school to help solve our clients' problems. You may remember I-RAC, C-RAC, or CREAC, among other legal analysis formats, from your law school days. No matter what legal analysis format you are familiar with, you can still use the basic idea of applying the law to the facts of the case to help your clients.

So, after we have actively listened, and after we have worked on understanding our clients' goals, values, and feelings, we can move to the analysis portion of the interview. During this part of the interview, we begin to identify and describe potential legal issues related to our clients' stories. We may begin to propose potential solutions to our clients' problems, and we can discuss the risks and benefits related to these solutions. Finally, we may begin to outline additional work that we may need to perform in order to best represent our clients.

A. Applying the Law or Preparing a Research Strategy to Find the Law

I should first say that we might not always have the opportunity to provide some legal analysis in our initial client interviews. For one thing, we may not have enough information on our clients' cases before they walk into our offices for the interviews. If we don't have much information on their cases, we may not even know what law would be applicable for the legal application. Secondly, even if we do have sufficient information on our clients' cases before the initial client interview, we may not have had sufficient time to perform any substantive research on the applicable law before the clients come into our offices. So, remember to be flexible. Some of our legal analysis may take place in later interviews with our clients. Indeed, legal analysis will take place throughout the course of our representation of our clients. New facts may emerge. Laws may be modified. As the late and great singer *David Bowie* might say, *Ch-Ch-Ch-Ch-Changes* may happen that require us to reanalyze and reevaluate our clients' cases.

1. *We Are Lawyers. So Let's Find and Work with the Law!*

In situations where we have not had enough time or information to perform any substantive research related to our clients' cases, we can still use our initial client interviews as an opportunity to discuss with our clients any research that we plan to perform relating to their cases. As we listen to our clients' stories, we may begin to identify some issues that might be legally relevant. Whether it is our attorney intuition or our prior experience with a similar case, we can tell our clients what research we plan to perform relating to their cases.

Let's look at an exchange where the attorney identifies a potential legal issue and proposes a research plan. As you read the exchange, try to also identify where the attorney uses reflection and empathy:

Attorney:	Mrs. Morrison, you mentioned that your son, Jake, has been told by school administration that he cannot wear his denim jacket to school because it is distracting and violates a school dress code policy.
Client:	Yes. It's ridiculous! Jake wore the jacket to school the other day, and he was sent to the principal's office. The Assistant Principal for Discipline told Jake that he had to take off his jacket and leave it in his locker for the rest of the day. He was also told that he could get suspended for wearing the jacket at school again! Jake was embarrassed and a little scared. But, most of all, he was mad that he could not wear the jacket that he spent his own money on to school. He worked for that money! He wants to wear that jacket!
Attorney:	Interesting. Well, I can tell that you are quite upset with the situation.
Client:	I am!

Attorney:	Well, Mrs. Morrison, it sounds like there may be some First Amendment/Free Speech issues going on here. You've made it quite clear that Jake is not satisfied with the school's request that he no longer wear his jacket at school.
Client:	Absolutely! He wants to wear the jacket that he bought with his own money! It's not like there are curse words or nasty pictures on the jacket. It just has a few pictures of some of the musicians that he likes to listen to.
Attorney:	Okay. Well, I understand that Jake really wants to wear his jacket. It sounds like he is quite proud to have been able to buy that jacket with his own money. But, at this point, I'd suggest that he hold off on wearing the jacket—at least, just for a few days. You see. I am not quite familiar with the law relating to school dress code policies and a student's right to freedom of speech and expression in a public school. I can tell you that, generally, there are rights to free speech and free expression. But, these rights do have limitations.
Client:	Okay.
Attorney:	So, like I said, I haven't taken a look at these legal issues in a while. What I propose is that you give me a couple of days to do a little legal research. Let me do a little research on what schools can and cannot do in restricting a

	student's ability to wear certain clothing at a public school. In the meantime, perhaps, you might be able to provide me with the school policy that the Assistant Principal told Jake that he violated?
Client:	Okay. Yes. The Assistant Principal wrote down the policy number on a piece of paper and handed it to Jake. And I think the policy is on the school's website. I'll email you the policy number and the website when I get back home this afternoon.
Attorney:	Good. So, I'll review the school policy and do a little legal research. I'll also need to talk to Jake. I plan to tell him to hold off on wearing the jacket while I work on this research.
Client:	Yes. That seems fine, because I don't want my boy getting suspended!
Attorney:	Great. I wouldn't want my child getting suspended either.

* * *

You will notice that the attorney in the above example was honest with Mrs. Morrison in his lack of knowledge relating to First Amendment issues. He provided what little information that he may have remembered from his law school Constitutional Law class. He reflected back to Mrs. Morrison some of the factual content and emotions relating to her son's legal problem. And then he suggested a research plan that might help answer the problem.

2. *It's Legal Analysis. But, Don't Promise Results You Can't Deliver!*

It is never good to promise results that we can't deliver—especially in an initial meeting with our clients. We don't want to raise our clients' expectations just to watch them sink like the Titanic when we provide our clients with bad news. If we don't know how the law will apply to our clients' facts, then we should hold off on advising the clients of any legal application. Slow down. Don't try to start providing answers, when you don't know how to answer the question. If we are missing a big piece of information from that word problem, and that missing piece is the law, we should go find the law. We should research the law. We should update the law. Then, we can apply it to our clients' facts.

When we apply the law to our clients' facts—especially in our earlier client interviews—we similarly should not promise results that we can't deliver. Unless we are hoping to examine the extent of our malpractice coverage, we shouldn't guarantee an outcome. Words like "generally," "usually," "typically," or "often" might help us out. Here are some less than surefire phrases that we may consider using when we frame our legal analysis of our clients' cases to our clients:

- "In situations like yours, what normally happens is this . . . "

- "What the court usually examines in these cases is . . . "

- "Generally, the court will find that . . . "

- "Most often, we are looking at . . . "

B. Discussion of Potential Solutions to the Clients' Problems

After we have had an opportunity to provide some legal analysis to our clients, we may want to explore some potential solutions to our clients' problems. Let's explore discussing potential solutions with our clients.

1. *It's the Client's Choice*

After we have had an initial discussion on any potential legal issues that may be related to our clients' problems, we can move forward and begin a conversation on potential solutions related to these legal issues.

During this portion of the interview, we can begin discussions on any legal rights and responsibilities related to our clients' problems. We can begin to brainstorm on a variety of approaches to resolving our clients' problems. And we can describe to the clients any potential risks and benefits related to these approaches to resolving our clients' problems. These approaches may include "legal" and "non-legal" alternatives.

But, while we are providing our advice and counsel to our clients, we should be cognizant of what the clients have told us with respect to *their* goals, values, and expectations. We should ask our clients how the proposed solutions to their problems match up with what *they want* to get out of their cases—for example, financially, physically, and emotionally. After all, we are only advising our clients on what possible solutions may be out there related to their problems. Our clients are the decision-makers. Even though we may have been trying to walk in our clients' shoes throughout the client interview, we can't speak for our clients. No matter how strong our ventriloquist skills may be, we need to let our clients speak for themselves. They decide what is right for them.

2. *Discussion of Possible "Legal" and "Non-Legal" Options*

So, after we have identified some initial legal issues and found and applied the law to the facts of our clients' cases, we may have an opportunity to explore possible solutions to our clients' problems. And when I say "solutions," I don't mean that we are always going to have the perfect answer to our clients' problems. Yes, there is usually a correct answer to a math problem. Even those math word problems that I have been talking about for most of the book have a correct answer. But, it's not the same with the law. You may have heard that the law is not always black and white. We can't just turn to the back of a book and find the single answers that solve our clients' problems. There is a lot of grey in the law. There is often a range of possible solutions to a legal problem: some very good solutions; some not quite good, but still acceptable solutions; and some absolutely undesirable solutions.

Think about it. How often did your law professors say something like "It depends" in class? There are many facts, nuances, values, motivations, and strategies that go into play when exploring possible solutions to our clients' problems. Some of our exploration will go down the "legal" side. After all, we are lawyers. We studied the law. Our clients come talk to us because we should know the law or know where to find the law.

Solutions on the "legal" side are often litigation-based or involve some court intervention. They can encompass a variety of options that we, as lawyers, may be more comfortable identifying:

filing a lawsuit; seeking an injunction; requesting monetary damages; paying restitution; terminating a contract; suppressing certain evidence. The list can go on and on. These legal solutions are no doubt important. They help protect our clients' rights. They help provide an answer to many of our clients' problems.

But we should remember that "non-legal" solutions might also help answer our clients' problems. Now, these solutions are not against the law—that is not what makes them "non-legal" in my eyes. Non-legal solutions are just not ligation-based. They don't require some court intervention or approval. Yet, they may still help answer our clients' problems. So, don't be afraid to explore non-legal options, like writing a letter to an opposing party or proposing an informal settlement conference. These options may be particularly enticing for clients who fear a long, drawn out legal battle.

Yes, clients seek us out because we are lawyers. We work with the law, and we sometimes go to court. But, as we listen to our clients' stories, we can begin to identify what options may be best suited for them. Not every client will want a court battle. Not every client will need a harsh or litigious encounter. Some clients may be able to receive a satisfactory result for their legal problems with minimal or no court involvement. Some may even just want a heartfelt apology from the other side. So, pay attention to your clients and be willing to explore legal and non-legal options.

Now, let's revisit the Mrs. Morrison free speech hypothetical. As you read the exchange, take a look at how the attorney provided some legal application and presented some legal and non-legal solutions to the situation with her son and his jacket:

* * *

Attorney:	Mrs. Morrison, we have done some initial legal research on a public school's ability to prevent a student from wearing certain clothing at school. As you know, we have also had a chance to speak to Jake. And, he is okay with me talking to you about my research and the possible options moving forward.
Client:	Yes.
Attorney:	So, as I had initially mentioned, we do have a right to freedom of speech and a right to express ourselves as we see fit. This right also applies to students in public schools. But, as I also mentioned, these rights are not absolute. There are certain limitations that can be placed on our rights to free speech and to free expression. And one of these limitations relates to *where* we want to speak or express ourselves.
Client:	Okay. So can Jake wear the jacket to school or not?
Attorney:	Well, it would appear that the school might have the right to limit what Jake can wear at school. I mentioned that one of the limitations to our rights to free speech and expression relates to where we want to speak or express ourselves. Public school administrators may generally set certain dress code policies—and, thereby, restrict students from wearing certain types of clothing—*if* the policies are applied to *all* students across the board and *if* the policies

are considered "content neutral"—which means that the policies don't only restrict certain types of messages on the clothing. Here, it looks like the school's policy restricts all students from wearing clothing that displays or identifies any type of a musician's work. So, it doesn't look like the policy is favoring one type of musician over another, or one type of message over another.

Client: Okay.

Attorney: So, like I said, this information is based on our initial research into the matter. And like I told Jake, we are happy to perform some additional research for him, and we are happy to move forward with some additional work on this matter for him.

Client: But, how long would that take? We don't really have time to be worrying about a lawsuit. And, Jake is a senior already. He'll be graduating from high school in a few months.

Attorney: Well, it is difficult to say how long it would take to work through this matter. As I told Jake, we could reach out to the school and see if the school would be willing to modify its dress code policy. But, I suspect that the school would not just quickly agree to change its policy—especially towards the end of a school year. We could threaten litigation—take the school to court and argue that the policy is unconstitutional. But, my

	initial read of the law seems to support a school's general ability to make and enforce similar dress code policies.
Client:	And, I imagine that a lawsuit could take more time and cost more money.
Attorney:	Well, yes. With more work, there would definitely be additional costs. And, you are right. A lawsuit would take some time. And I know you said that you and Jake don't have the time to worry about a lawsuit—much less a lengthy lawsuit. And, as you mentioned, Jake is graduating in a few months.
Client:	Yeah. I am not sure we would want to pursue any legal action. I just don't think it would be good for us right now.
Attorney:	I understand, Mrs. Morrison. It sounds like you and Jake are on the same page. Jake told me that it was okay to tell you that he is not interested in pursuing legal action.
Client:	Is there anything else that we might be able to do?
Attorney:	Well, I guess we could reach out to the school to see if Jake would be allowed to wear his jacket inside out. I talked to Jake about wearing his jacket inside out, and he said that he would be okay with that—as long as he wouldn't get suspended. He also said that he would be okay with me talking to you about this.

Client:	Wear his jacket inside out? What do you mean?
Attorney:	Well, you mentioned that Jake really wanted to wear the jacket that he purchased with his own money to school. The dress code policy seems to be most concerned with the *displaying* of the messages. In other words, the policy doesn't restrict students from wearing denim jackets. If the jacket is worn inside out, the messages are less likely to be displayed. He may not be violating the dress code policy if he wears the jacket inside out.
Client:	I see. So, Jake could still get to wear the jacket. He just would not be showing the message. I can see why Jake would be okay with that. I have seen him wear his sweatshirts and T-shirts inside out sometimes. So, it would not seem that unusual for him to wear a jacket inside out.
Attorney:	Well, great. Let me reach out to the Assistant Principal of Discipline and seek some clarification on the policy. I'll let her know that I have spoken to you and Jake, and that Jake would like to wear his jacket inside out. I will let Jake know what I hear back from her.
Client:	Great.

* * *

In the above example, the attorney tried to provide some explanation of how the law applied to the facts of the case (or, he provided a summarization of the explanation that he had provided to Jake). As the fifth pillar to the conversation foundation suggests, the attorney first tried to explain, in layman's terms, a student's First Amendment right to freedom of speech and freedom of expression in a public school. Then the attorney applied the law to the facts of the case—also in layman's terms. Finally, the attorney discussed some possible legal and non-legal solutions with Mrs. Morrison that he had previously explored with Jake.

Mrs. Morrison expressed some concerns about a long and potentially expensive court battle, and Jake indicated that he did not want to pursue legal action. On top of these concerns, the initial legal research showed a possible uphill battle challenging the school's ability to restrict the type of clothing that students wear at the school. As a result, the attorney explored a non-legal option that was somewhat satisfactory to Jake (and his mother, as well). The non-legal option, while not the best possible solution to the legal problem, still touched on some of the major goals and emotions that were expressed in the interviews with Jake and his mother. In the vast greyness of possible answers to the legal problem, wearing a jacket inside out turned out to be an acceptable shade of grey.

C. Identifying Further Steps

The analysis portion of the client interview can also provide an opportunity for us to identify documents to review and further individuals to interview.

While we are discussing our research plan or legal strategy for our clients' cases, we can create a list of documents that we would need to obtain and review to further help analyze our clients' problems. We can discuss with our clients what documents we expect them to provide to us and what documents that we can locate ourselves. Likewise, we can use this portion of the interview to identify and get the contact information for other individuals that we may want to speak to in order to gain a better picture of the situations relating to our clients' problems.

CHAPTER 17

Shutting It Down! Closure Is Good, Even in a Client Interview

If you have ever experienced a relationship breakup and don't understand why the breakup even occurred, you can appreciate the benefits of closure.

Concluding a client interview with some closure helps our clients feel like the professional relationship that they have established with us is still positive. It makes them feel like they *have been* AND *still are* an integral part to the relationship. Why would we work so hard at establishing trust and rapport with our clients just to suddenly end the interview like a heartbreaking last-second shot that helps a team lose a hard-fought championship basketball game? Like the players on the losing team, our clients would wonder if there was anything else they could have done to help prolong the interview or change the sudden outcome. Why would we want to practice our active listening skills and empathize with what our clients are going through, but not care how our clients feel when they leave our office? No. We have worked too hard with our client interviews to end them this way. We should also work on providing closure.

Just like the roadmap of the client interview that we discussed in Chapter 14 helped outline what we could say during the client interview, our closing for our client interviews can follow a general format that outlines what we might be able to say at the end of our client interviews. This closure outline can summarize what we discussed with our clients during the interview and what we plan to do moving forward with our representation. Here are four steps that we might consider including in the closure part of our client interviews:

- First, when we begin to conclude our interview, we want to thank our clients for having taken the time to speak with us.

- Second, we should remind our clients of what the next steps will be in our representation of them. For example, we may let our clients know that we are going to conduct some research on their cases and report back to them in a certain period of time.

- Third, we want to be clear with our clients as to what we can expect *them* to do to assist us in our representation of them. For example, if our clients need to get a specific document to us, we can remind them what document they need to provide and when we can expect to receive it.

- Finally, we can let our clients know of our availability for further conversations or questions.

Let's visit another client interview. As you read the exchange, try to identify whether the attorney touches on these four closure points:

* * *

Attorney:	Mr. Riley, our hour-long interview is almost over. But, this interview is just the beginning of our work for you.
Client:	Yes. I understand.
Attorney:	We want to thank you, again, for coming in to talk to us. We certainly appreciated getting to hear and understand a little more about your situation with your neighbor's loud music. Like I said earlier, I am going to do a little research on nuisance laws, and how they might relate to your situation.
Client:	Yes. Okay.
Attorney:	And while we are working on that research, you indicated that you would work on providing us the email that you sent to your neighbors. You said that you could provide us the email by the end of the week.
Client:	Yes. I will forward you the email tomorrow.
Attorney:	Great. So, we will report back to you the results of our legal research in a couple of days. After the research is completed, we can plan on scheduling another office meeting to discuss what other options we might explore with this matter.

Client:	Sounds like a good plan.
Attorney:	Wonderful. Well, are there any other questions that you may have at this time? Or, anything else that you would like to share with us at this time?
Client:	No. I think you answered all my questions. And, I really appreciate you spending some time with me.
Attorney:	Great. Well, thanks again for coming in to see us, Mr. Riley. Feel free to reach out to us if you have any questions on what is going on with this case, or if you have anything else you would like for us to know. You can email either of us, and we will try to respond to you as soon as we can.
Client:	Thank you so much.
Attorney:	Thank you, Mr. Riley. Have a wonderful afternoon.

* * *

Notice how the attorney in the above example allowed for some time to close the interview. The attorney did not just quickly say she had to leave. She did not drop the interview like a hot potato. She thanked the client for coming in to see her. She outlined what her office was going to do on the file and what Mr. Riley was expected to do to assist in the representation. And she let Mr. Riley know of her availability via email. She provided closure to the initial interview.

I should reiterate that is not necessary that we get every single piece of information that we wanted to get out of the interview *in just one* interview. With the trust and rapport that we have worked on building during the interview, we should feel comfortable reaching out to the clients if we need additional information from them or further clarification on some facts that were described in their stories. In fact, we will often need more than one interview to get the necessary information from our clients to best represent them. Therefore, we should not feel pressured to continue the interview beyond the time that we have allotted for the interview. It is okay to stop. There are telephone calls, text and email messages, and future office meetings where we can continue to speak with our clients. We can extend our interviewing and counseling of our clients beyond our initial client interviews.

Now, let's extend our reading to Part 5 of the book. Part 5 provides a summary of some basic counseling skills that you might be able to use when you interview and counsel your clients.

You Don't Have to Be an Experienced Therapist to Practice Basic Client Counseling Skills

I started this book by talking about how my law license says that I am an attorney *and* counselor. And, yes. Your law license likely says that you are an attorney *and* counselor, too.

If our law licenses say that we are attorneys *and* counselors, then we should try to embrace the counseling aspect of our jobs. Part 5 of this book describes some basic counseling skills that we can use as we embrace our jobs as attorneys *and* counselors. You will notice that some of these counseling skills have already been discussed and demonstrated in Parts 3 and 4 of this book. Like a good counselor, I have tried to emphasize key points by repeating them multiple times throughout the book. I have tried to model some of the behavior that I hope you will consider doing as you embrace your jobs as attorneys *and* counselors.

CHAPTER 18

Training as an Attorney and Counselor: An Introduction

A. Accept It and Embrace It. Counseling Is Part of Our Jobs

Counseling is a big part of what we do as attorneys. Our clients often rely on us to help counsel them through some of the most significant parts of their lives. Our work can touch the hopes, dreams, safety, and livelihood of our clients.

But, many of us forget to focus on the counseling aspect of our jobs. Like a nervous child in a preschool before he has to show and tell his stuffed bear, we shy away from talking to our clients about their concerns, goals, and values. We focus on "THE LAW" and "LEGAL ANALYSIS." But, we sometimes forget that there are people, companies, and organizations that are directly impacted by the work that we do. And, what about the F-word? Well, many of us neglect to talk to our clients about their *feelings*. And we hardly remember to acknowledge that *our* thoughts and feelings can influence the work that we do for our clients as well. We need to accept and embrace that we are attorneys *and* counselors.

B. Varying the Level of Our "Counseliness"

Now the level of "counseliness" that we use in our client interviews will vary depending on our clients' level of education, sophistication, and familiarity with attorneys. Yes. I just made up a word: "counseliness." It's the amount of counseling skills that attorneys will use during the course of a client interview. It could also rack you up some good points on a *Scrabble* game!

The more educated, sophisticated, or familiar that our clients are with working with attorneys, the fewer counseling skills that we may need to employ. These types of clients may not need us to be as "touchy-feely" when we are working with them in our professional relationship. For example, we may be working with a general counsel who is educated and familiar with lawsuits or legal transactions. General counsel understand legal analysis and frequently work with other attorneys to identify the risks and benefits associated with a lawsuit or legal transaction. Indeed, the very purpose for a general counsel position is often to help serve a company's legal department, and many general counsel, if not all of them, are licensed attorneys.

For these particularly sophisticated clients, the legal problems that they present to us may not be that stressful to them because they deal with legal problems on a daily basis. As such, the counseling skills that we use during interviews with sophisticated clients may not be as important to the overall effectiveness of the client interview and our professional relationship with them. In other words, our level of "counseliness" with these types of clients may not have to be that high.

Nevertheless, for many other clients—particularly those clients who have never met or worked with an attorney before— this one legal problem that they are facing may be the most important and stressful part of their lives. However small their legal problems may seem *to us*, these clients may carry their problems like a huge burden on their shoulders. They may be overcome with worry, and they may fear speaking to an attorney. These anxieties may create roadblocks to the requisite information that we need to best represent our clients. We will need to employ a higher level of "counseliness" when working with these types of clients.

We can use some basic counseling skills in our interviews with inexperienced or anxious clients to help acquire the information that we need to help serve them. Some of these same skills have already been discussed and demonstrated in Parts 3 and 4 of the book. Part 5 of the book further examines some of these skills (and other skills!) in Chapters 19-24. As you read Chapters 19-24 of the book, think about why an attorney may want to develop some of these counseling skills. If you can identify the counseling skills and understand the reasons why we may want to use them in a client interview, then you are already becoming a better attorney *and* counselor!

CHAPTER 19

Be Ready, Genuine, and Present

A. Ready. Set. Focus!

Let's face it. Almost everyone we know lives a busy life. We have so much going on in our everyday lives that it is sometimes hard to focus on one thing. We praise ourselves when we can successfully multitask. We worry about wasting time. We get distracted.

Attorneys often also multitask. We can also waste our time. And, yes. We can get distracted, too.

An attorney's distraction can be one of the most frustrating aspects for our clients during a client interview. Clients don't appreciate our inattentiveness. They don't want us to be preoccupied with some other task or easily sidetracked from *their* designated time with us. They rightfully prefer us to be focused and present in the professional relationship. So, check those emails and answer those text messages before you walk into the client interview.

It can be quite difficult to remove the thoughts and feelings that we have related to our daily lives and *be genuinely present* during our client interviews. It can be equally challenging to eliminate any personal judgment and biases that we may have about our clients or their problems—and simply concentrate on what our clients are presenting to us. Yet, like an Olympic archer who has to remain focused during her archery event, we should strive to stay focused on our clients when we interview them. If we are able to do so, our clients will feel more comfortable telling us their complete stories. And they will feel more confident that we will understand their stories.

B. Don't Fake It! Be Genuine

Our clients want us to stay focused on their legal problems. They want us to remain attentive to their work. And they want us to show them that we are following and understanding their stories. They also want us to be ourselves. They want us to be genuine.

Clients can tell when we don't want to be there in the conference room speaking to them. They can tell when we are more concerned with something outside the conference room. They can read body language just the same as we can. They can listen to the tone of our voice just like we can listen to the tone of their voice. So, we can't fake it when we speak to our clients. They will call us out, and we may not even be focused enough to respond. They will shut down and stop giving us the information that we need to best serve them in their cases.

So, let's try to remain genuine in the way we speak to and act with our clients. Let's try to stay cognizant of what is happening to us *internally* when our clients are speaking to us.

What are we thinking or feeling during the course of the interview? Do our thoughts stray to matters unrelated to the very client that is before us? Are any of our personal biases or prejudgments clouding our understanding of what the clients are telling us?

If we are aware of what *we* are thinking and feeling as our clients tell us their stories, then we are more likely to ensure that there is congruency between what we do and say. We are more likely to make sure that what we are telling our clients matches up with our nonverbal behavior. When we do this, we are better able to identify and remedy any barriers that we may be building into the professional relationship.

As *Oprah Winfrey* might say, let's try to remain our "authentic selves" when we speak to our clients. And if our authentic selves are too tired or preoccupied with something other than the client waiting in the conference room, then we should not simply fake it. We can acknowledge to ourselves what we are thinking and feeling, and we can proactively do something that counters some of our distraction. Subpart C below provides some suggestions that we can do to help remove some of these distractions before we enter the conference room.

C. Proactively Try to Counter Your Distractions

If we are feeling a little too tired or preoccupied to speak to our clients, we may be lucky enough to be able to reschedule the client interview with no harm and no foul. But, not all of us can be that fortunate. So, if we are faced with the dilemma of having to interview and counsel a client when our heads are not quite focused on that client, take a quick mini-break before you walk into the conference room. This may sound cliché, but do something to clear your mind and wake yourself up.

I was a big "power-napper" in college. A little 10-minute snooze on my small bunk bed in the afternoon would help me get through some of those long days of work, studying, and, yes— "fun." The naps would revitalize me. I would wake up more refreshed and ready to tackle another collegiate "challenge."

Now I am not advocating that you sleep on the job at your work—especially if your work is not really *your* law office work. You are much more likely to get into some trouble if you are sleeping on the job when your last name is not on the firm letterhead, if you know what I mean. But, a quick 5-minute relaxation moment where you take a few deep breaths might provide some revitalization. Perhaps, you can throw a few arm or neck stretches in the mix. Or, you can take a short 5-10 minute walk in the fresh air.

Any of these quick activities might put us in a different frame of mind before our client interviews. Not all of us can or will want to throw some fresh water on our faces. And not all of us are capable of downing canister after canister of coffee. So, a few moments where we can reconvene ourselves may be the best alternative. We may not be taking a 10-minute power nap on an uncomfortable mattress in a smelly college dormitory, but we may still be ready to tackle another challenge after we have given ourselves a quick little "me time."

CHAPTER 20

Don't Shut Down the Conversation from the Get-Go: Open with Open-Ended Questions

A. The Benefits of Open-Ended Questions

We have already spent some time discussing the benefits of starting our fact-gathering portion of our client interviews with open-ended questions. Parts 3 and 4 of the book discussed and demonstrated how open-ended questions encourage our clients to *openly* tell their stories. Open-ended questions tell clients that we want to listen to and understand what they know, think, and feel about their problems. They encourage clients to *explain* their narratives.

Parts 3 and 4 of the book provided examples of how opened-ended and closed-ended questions can influence our client interviews. You may have noticed some similarities with the questions that were asked.

- Close-ended questions typically begin with the words:

  - Is

  - Did

  - Are

  - Were

  - Who

  - When

  - Where

- Open-ended questions typically begin with the words:

  - How

  - What

  - Why

Although not ideal for the first question in an initial client interview, here's one of the most common and effective forms of an open-ended question: "What happened next?" This question helps the clients to think chronologically. It helps clients frame their stories in the order that the stories occurred. Non-verbal cues, like a nod of the head or an "Mm-hmm," can also encourage our clients to continue their narratives without the interference of any preconceptions that we may have relating to what may or may not be important.

Here are few other ways to "ask" an open-ended question without creating any unnecessary interference on our part. Notice that with this list below, we are "asking" an open-ended question without really asking a question:

- "Tell me more."

- "I see."

- "Go on."

- "Okay."

- "Interesting."

- "Help me understand a little more about what may have happened."

B. We Can Still Be Friends with Close-Ended Questions

If asked too early in a client interview, closed-ended questions might shut down the interview by limiting what our clients can tell us about their legal problems. Close-ended questions don't encourage clients to fully explain themselves as they tell us their stories. Close-ended questions tell clients that short and quick answers (often one- or two-word answers!) are enough to give us the information that we need to help solve their legal problems.

Even though we may want to limit our close-ended questions at the start of our client interviews, we should still keep close-ended questions handy. We will want to ask close-ended questions to help us understand any information from our clients' stories that needs clarification. Close-ended questions can help us focus our clients on the particular parts of their stories that we may feel are most relevant to the legal issues that their stories present. Like a great coffee filter, close-ended questions can help us sift through some of the tangential information that our clients can present to us in their stories. This can be particularly beneficial during work stretches when we have little or no time for extended chats. So, close-ended questions are good. They are our friends. Just don't bring your friends out so early in the client interview.

CHAPTER 21

This Is Not Physical Education, but Practice Active Listening

A. Can You Hear Me? Active Listening Is Hard

I noted earlier in the book that active listening is hard. We like to hear ourselves speak. And our clients seek us out for our legal advice. So, our clients want to hear us speak, too. But, we won't have much to talk about if we don't first actively listen to our clients' stories.

Clients appreciate when we are actively engaged in their interviews. Even though our clients want to hear our legal advice, they often need time to express themselves—to tell their stories. They need time to *advise us* on what we are going to be *advising them* about. And as they advise us on their legal problems, we should actively listen.

Active listening is difficult because it is <u>way</u> more than just hearing our clients speak. When we are actively listening, we allow our clients to tell their stories, AND *we receive their stories*. We maintain good eye contact with our clients, and we patiently listen to the facts that help us identify the "who," "what," "when," "where," "how," and "why" of our clients' stories. We listen for our clients' goals, values, and expectations related to their stories. And we listen and try to understand any emotional context that our clients may present to us as they discuss their stories.

So, yes, active listening is hard. We can't be successful client interviewers by simply doing the equivalent of skim reading or scanning a text. We can't get all the information that we need to help serve our clients if we don't actively listen. But, good news! The work that we put into actively listening will be used later in the client interview. We will use the information that we picked up as we actively listened to our clients when we summarize, reflect, and empathize.

B. More than Words: Pay Attention to Nonverbal Clues

So, active listening is hard. We have to listen to a variety of things that our clients are telling us. Facts? Goals? Values? Expectations? Emotions? Yes. We have to pay attention to all of those things. Let me add one more thing that we should pay attention to as we actively listen: our clients' nonverbal behavior.

I mentioned in Chapter 8 that we should pay attention to the way we say things to our clients and the way we act in front of our clients. I noted that we should pay attention to the tone of our voice and our emoji. Well, we should also pay attention to our clients' tone of voice and their emoji. Let's actively listen to our clients' nonverbal communication!

Yes. We can listen to nonverbal cues. As our clients tell us their stories, we should pay attention to their eye contact, posture, facial expressions, and gestures. Do our clients look away as they are detailing a particular fact of their stories? Do they slouch? Are they covering part of their face with their arm? Do they smile? Laugh? Tremble?

These nonverbal cues that our clients present to us during their stories may be just as important as the facts of the stories themselves. These nonverbal cues further help paint the picture of what our clients are going through. Like a topping on an ice cream cone, they add something else to the mix. They provide more meaning to what the clients have already told us. They help provide more context to the clients' stories. They provide more flavor.

Now, flavor can mean different things to different folks. What may seem salty or spicy to you may seem bland or mild to me. So, as we actively listen to our clients and observe their nonverbal behavior, we should not presume to automatically understand what our clients' nonverbal behavior means. There may be cultural, age, or factual differences that impact how our clients express themselves nonverbally. For example, if our clients are maintaining good eye contact as they speak with us, they *generally* may be indicating to us that they are being attentive and speaking honestly. However, for some cultures, maintaining eye contact may be an indication of disrespect. There may be cultural differences that impact how and whether a client maintains eye contact.

So, we should try to pay attention to the nonverbal cues that our clients present to us as we interview and counsel them. We should take note when our clients' behavior or tone of voice changes as they tell us their stories or as they listen to our counsel. But, we should not presume to automatically understand every nonverbal cue that our clients present to us. If we are actively listening to the information that our clients express verbally and nonverbally, and if we have been working hard to establish trust and rapport, then we should feel confident in using the interview session as an opportunity to ask additional questions that may help clarify the picture that the clients are painting for us—both with their words and nonverbal behavior.

C. Mirror Some of the Clients' Nonverbal Behavior

As we listen to and try to understand our clients' nonverbal cues, we should try to mirror some of what they are doing. Now, I am not talking about copying everything that our clients do. That type of mimicry would be weird and creepy.

Mirroring simply means trying to match *some* of our nonverbal behavior with our clients' nonverbal behavior. Mirroring is a technique that may help build trust and rapport with our clients, because the clients can see that we receive and identify some of the nonverbal cues that they are displaying. It may help put our clients a little more at ease, because they might feel somewhat of a nonverbal connection to us.

For example, if our clients are speaking to us in a soft tone of voice when they tell us their stories, then we should similarly try to speak in a softer tone of voice back to our clients. Speaking back to our clients loudly and aggressively when they are speaking to us in a soft and passive manner could create some barriers to our professional relationship with our clients. The clients would begin to think that we are not listening to and understanding what they are saying. They would begin to think that we don't get them. The same barriers could also develop if we joyfully or comically spoke back to our clients when they are speaking to us in a distraught or depressed manner.

Likewise, if our clients are leaning forward on their chairs when they are speaking to us, then we may want to similarly lean forward on our chairs. When our clients lean forward on their chairs when they are speaking to us, they may be providing us with several nonverbal cues that we may want to mirror. They may be showing us that they feel like what they are speaking about is important. They may be telling us that they want and need to be heard. They may be telling us that the problems that they are discussing with us are so pressing for them that they can't lean back and relax on their chairs.

We should pay attention to our clients' nonverbal cues and try to mirror some of what the clients may be telling us. If they are showing us that they are trying to attentively sit up on their chairs as they speak of some important matters, then we, too, should try to attentively sit up on our chairs as we receive their information and provide our legal counsel. However, we should be careful not to mirror some client nonverbal cues that could indicate to our clients that we are unwilling to help them. For example, if our clients' arms are crossed over their chests as we speak to them, they _generally_ may be indicating to us that they may not fully trust us or be open to our counsel. If we mirrored back this nonverbal behavior, our arms crossed over our chests could indicate to our clients that we are frustrated with the attorney-client relationship, suspicious of what the clients have said, or hopeful that the interview time will end soon so that we can leave the office and do something more productive and satisfying.

Likewise, if our clients spoke to us in an angry or screaming tone of voice, we would want to remain calm and not mirror this tone of voice back to our clients. Screaming at our clients or coming across as angry at them—especially in our initial client interviews—would obviously shut down any trust or rapport that may have already been established. It might also frighten some of the other folks in our office space!

So, pick and choose what nonverbal cues you want to mirror back to your clients. If you feel that the mirroring of your clients' nonverbal cues would help move the professional relationship forward, then mirror away. If you feel that your mirroring would hinder the professional relationship, then **put** the mirror away.

CHAPTER 22

You've Listened to the Client's Story. Make Sure You Got It Right: Summarize and Reflect!

After we have allowed the clients to tell their stories, it is important that we summarize back to our clients what we heard them say. Now, if you are able to summarize everything word-for-word back to the clients, good for you! But, a verbatim summarization is not needed, and it is not effective. We can still build rapport with our clients and ensure that we have an accurate understanding of the information that they have provided to us by simply paraphrasing some of the major details of their stories. So, as Parts 3 and 4 of the book described and illustrated, take some time to summarize. Reflect back to the clients the *factual content* AND *emotional context* of their stories. You can often start your summarization with these phrases:

- "It sounds like . . . "

- "It appears like . . . "

- "From what I gather . . . "

- "As I understand it . . . "

A. Mirror, Mirror: Reflect Back the Factual Content of the Clients' Stories

As we summarize our clients' stories, we want to reflect back to our clients the factual information that they have discussed with us. It is important that we have a good understanding of the factual details related to our clients' stories. As Chapter 9 noted, the factual details of our clients' stories may play key parts in our legal analysis. They may determine how we ultimately evaluate our clients' cases.

Imagine defending a car accident case and not knowing whether your client thought the light was red, green, or yellow as he proceeded through the intersection. This is a key fact that we would need to know about in a personal injury car accident case. This is a key fact that we would want our clients to discuss with us during the client interview. This is a key fact that we would want to reflect back to the clients to ensure that we have an accurate understanding of what happened at the time of the accident.

We want to make sure that we have a good understanding of any factual detail that we think *may* ultimately impact the outcome of our clients' cases. We want to make sure that we have a good understanding of any facts that our clients tell us that go to the heart of what the clients' legal problems may be about. We also want to make sure that we have a good understanding of any parts of our clients' stories that may seem to contradict or be inconsistent with what they may have previously told us during the interview. We can use our handy close-ended questions to help clarify any of these details.

B. Mirror, Mirror: Reflect on Any Emotional Context Attached to the Clients' Stories

In addition to reflecting back to our clients any factual content related to their stories, we also want to make sure that we reflect back to our clients any emotional context attached to their stories. We want to summarize back to our clients any emotional cues that they may have directly or indirectly presented to us in their stories. As Chapter 9 noted, these emotional cues can help tell us what our clients think and feel about their legal problems. They can help paint a better picture of what our clients are going through. They can help us better understand our clients.

When we reflect back on the emotional context that our clients' stories present to us, we should often describe some emotion back to our clients! Since many of us shy away from the F-word, I figured I'd provide a non-exhaustive list of some *feelings* or emotions that our clients might present to us during our client interviews. We might be able to use some of these words to help summarize the emotional context attached to our clients' stories.

Here's the list (feel free to add to the list as you continue to become a better attorney *and* counselor!):

* * *

Happy	Confused	Distressed
Frustrated	Disgusted	Distracted
Upset	Intimidated	Misunderstood
Troubled	Victimized	Determined
Angered	Betrayed	Strengthened

Outraged	Hurt	Accepted
Annoyed	Nervous	Respected
Disappointed	Embarrassed	Relieved
Saddened	Anxious	Renewed
Offended	Frightened	Satisfied
Pleased	Overjoyed	Grateful
Optimistic	Confident	Surprised
Glad	Ecstatic	Inspired

* * *

C. Picking the Right Time to Summarize and Reflect

We don't want to summarize too soon in the client interview. It may take our clients a while to understand that we really do want them to speak. It may take them a while to appreciate that their stories are important to our professional relationship. It may take a while to develop that trust and rapport. So like a gardener who refuses to nip a flower bud that is just beginning its blossom, we don't want to cut off our clients too soon.

Before you get the urge to summarize, let the clients respond to some open-ended questions first. Give them an opportunity to relish their parts as storytellers. Don't automatically feel like you need to fill every moment of awkward silence with summarization. Silence can be a very useful tool that can encourage our clients to further elaborate on their stories.

When the information that our clients are providing begins to continually slow down, or if we notice that our clients have started to repeat a lot of what they have told us, then that might be an appropriate time to summarize some of the information. We may also want to summarize if we get into a situation where we have jotted down so many notes from our clients' stories that we are beginning to have some difficulty comprehending what they have told us. In these situations, incorporating some close-ended questions during our summary can help clarify some of this confusion.

Just like we sometimes pause a movie that we are watching to confirm with another viewer of the movie that we are correctly following the plot, we should feel comfortable hitting pause during the client interview to confirm with our clients that we are correctly following their stories. Parts 3 and 4 of the book provided examples of summarizing a client's story. Here is another example of how we might start the summarization portion of our client interview. As you read the exchange, see how the attorney sets the stage for the summarization of the factual content and emotional context of the client's story:

* * *

Attorney:	Thank you, Ms. Partridge. Thank you for spending some time telling us what has been going on with your ex-husband. We understand that it is not an easy story to tell. But, we appreciate that you are willing to be so specific with us regarding what has been happening with the custodial issues for your three children.

Client:	Well, you're welcome.
Attorney:	So, Ms. Partridge, you probably noticed that my paralegal and I were both taking notes while you were speaking. We take notes because we want to make sure that we get all the information that you are giving us in an accurate manner.
Client:	Yes. I understand.
Attorney:	Good. So, I am going to take a few minutes now to review some of these notes with you. I'll spend a little time summarizing some of the information that you just discussed with us. Please feel free to stop me if I misstate or misrepresent any of the information, or if you remember something new that we haven't had a chance to discuss yet. Because, like I said, we want to make sure that we have a good and accurate picture of what you have been going through.
Client:	Yes. I understand.
Attorney:	Good. So, you mentioned that . . . (attorney begins summarization).

* * *

Here's another example where an attorney reflects on some facts and emotion in the summarization. As you read the exchange, notice that the attorney asks clarifying questions during the summarization:

* * *

Attorney:	Mr. Perez, you seem quite shocked to find out that your father may have had a handwritten will.
Client:	I am. Dad never told me anything about a handwritten will. We were really close. I just don't understand why he wouldn't have told me something about it.
Attorney:	It must be difficult to not have an answer to that question. It sounds like you are still quite confused and hurt about discovering the handwritten will. Now, you mentioned that you were cleaning out your father's home when you discovered the will. You said the will was in his bedroom. Do you happen to remember where exactly in the bedroom the will was located? For example, did it happen to be in a desk? Or, in a safe? Or, in a dresser?

* * *

When we summarize the clients' stories, we can transition from open-ended to close-ended questions. We can move from questions that encourage our clients to tell their narratives to more close-ended questions that focus on particular details of the narratives. So, just because we are summarizing our clients' stories, it doesn't mean that our clients are not invited to speak. As the first example above provided, we can tell our clients to freely interrupt us if we misstated something or if they recall something that they want to add to their stories. As the second example demonstrated, we can also directly ask our clients questions during the summarization. These questions can be close-ended questions that point our clients to particular details of their stories that we need more information on. Like a second coat of paint on a wall, these clarifying questions help make our clients' stories richer, fuller, and more complete.

CHAPTER 23

I Understand. You Don't Have to Feel Sorry for Your Clients to Empathize

Summarization includes reflecting on the emotional context attached to our clients' stories. Part of this reflection includes our ability to identify our clients' feelings. Empathy includes *our understanding* of our clients' feelings.

Empathic attorneys try to understand what their clients are experiencing. They try to put themselves in their clients' shoes. Empathic attorneys ask themselves:

- What must it be like to see what my clients saw?

- What must it be like to feel what they felt?

- What must it sound like to hear what they heard?

- What must it be like to be them?

But it is not enough to internally ask these questions. It is not enough to just try to understand what our clients are going through. We need *to show* our clients that we understand what they are going through. We can help do this by showing empathy. We can convey our answers to these questions back to our clients with empathic responses. We can start off our empathic responses with phrases like "I imagine" or "It must be like."

We can better understand what our clients are going through when we try to appreciate their unique perspectives regarding their legal problems. If we are better able to understand what our clients are experiencing, then we can better identify and understand our clients' motivations and values. This helps us to better understand how potential legal or non-legal solutions can impact our clients' lives.

And as I mentioned in Chapter 10, empathy does not mean sympathy. We do not need to feel sorry for our clients to help understand what our clients are experiencing. We do not need to feel bad for our clients to still be supportive and effective attorneys.

The Power of "I Wonder"

Mental health professionals will tell you that the phrase "I wonder" can facilitate a therapeutic relationship. It allows a therapist to mildly propose options to a client without removing the client's autonomy or ability to make decisions.

"I wonder" is a helpful way to similarly make suggestions to our clients without removing their ability to make choices. It allows us to give legal advice on certain decisions that our clients will have to make without overly pressuring the clients to make the decisions we may think are best for them. This may seem a little bit confusing. *I wonder* if an example may help clarify how you might use the phrase "I wonder" in a client interview.

As you read the example below, try to also take note of the attorney's use of reflection and empathy, and how she begins to explain some of the substantive law in layman's terms. Consider this example as a summary of some of the main counseling skills that we have covered throughout the book:

* * *

Attorney:	Ms. Martin, I understand that you are hurt and frustrated with what has been happening at your home. You have had enough of your husband's infidelity. And you are ready to move on and get a divorce.
Client:	It can't come soon enough. I just want to make sure that I get full custody of my two boys. The boys need me. And I don't want them being raised by a no-good, lying, cheater.
Attorney:	I understand, Ms. Martin. It seems like you really love your children and want the best for them.
Client:	Yes. I do. I just don't want them going to my husband.
Attorney:	Yes, Ms. Martin. You have made it quite clear that you do not want your husband getting custody of your boys. So, let's talk a little about the custody issue.
Client:	Okay.
Attorney:	Great. Well, like I said, I can tell that you are a great, loving mother. I'm sure the boys are quite lucky to have you as their mom.
Client:	Thank you.
Attorney:	So, Ms. Martin. Sometimes—spouses who are going through a divorce—have a difficult time separating their strong feelings towards each other from how they feel their spouses are as parents and caregivers. They are so heated up,

	angered, and hurt that they may forget how much their children love their spouses and want to see their spouses.
Client:	Yeah. I can understand that.
Attorney:	I wonder if some of that might be going on here. And I bring this up, Ms. Martin, because the court will bring this up, too. As the good and concerned mother that you are, I want you to be prepared for what the court will want to know.
Client:	Okay. Yes. I want to be prepared.
Attorney:	The court will want to know how your husband is as a father—regardless of whether he cheated or not.
Client:	Okay.
Attorney:	The court will want to know how he has interacted with the boys. What kind of a relationship does he have with his sons? What kind of stuff does he do with them?
Client:	I see.
Attorney:	And, I know you may not want to hear this, but the court will likely want to allow your husband some custodial rights—meaning he will likely have the opportunity to see and visit with his sons.
Client:	Okay. Yes. I get it. I know that I am still reeling from the affair. And I know that my boys love their dad—even though I can't stand him right now.

Attorney:	Okay. Thank you for bringing that up. Divorces can get quite lengthy and messy. Emotions can get quite high, especially around custody issues. It is good to hear that you are able to separate some of your feelings towards your husband *as a husband* from your feelings towards him *as a father*. I wonder if your husband will be able to do the same.
Client:	Oh, I am sure he can. Just the other day, he was telling me how great I am with the kids. He told me that the kids love me and rely on me so much.
Attorney:	Great. I am sure his statements reaffirmed and validated your commitment to your sons.
Client:	They absolutely did. It was really good to hear how much he appreciates what I do for our children.

* * *

In the above example, the attorney used "I wonder" to introduce a potentially sensitive topic about parenting and custodial rights. Ms. Martin was obviously upset about her husband's infidelity. The attorney used "I wonder" to talk about how Ms. Martin felt about her husband as a father. The attorney acknowledged Ms. Martin's feelings of hurt and betrayal, while also gently moving the conversation along towards some discussion relating to how the boys felt about their dad and how the court would likely examine custody issues.

Notice also how the attorney sandwiched the "I wonder" statement between some positive reflective statements towards the client. The positive statements help ease the clients' ears towards something that is potentially not so positive. Ms. Martin initially noted quite adamantly that she did not want her boys seeing their father—a result the attorney knew quite well was likely not going to happen. Here are a couple of the reflective statements that the attorney told Ms. Martin that helped ease the conversation into a more realistic discussion about custodial options:

- "I understand, Ms. Martin. It seems like you really love your children and want the best for them."

- "Well, like I said, I can tell that you are a great, loving mother. I'm sure the boys are quite lucky to have you as their mom."

- "As the good and concerned mother that you are, I want you to be prepared for what the court will want to know."

- "It is good to hear that you are able to separate some of your feelings towards your husband *as a husband* from your feelings towards him *as a father*."

The attorney also used "I wonder" one more time in the conversation—to inquire about how the father felt about Ms. Martin as a mother. "I wonder" is also a useful way to introduce clarifying questions. The difficulty in using "I wonder" too often, though, is that we need to be careful that we are not simply leading our clients into their answers. We still need to practice our active listening skills. We still need to listen to what our clients are saying and observe what they are doing when they say it. We need to ask ourselves: Do our clients' answers to the "I wonder" statements fit in with their overall narrative? Do they seem out of place? Do our clients act or speak differently when they respond to our "I wonder" statements?

Our active listening skills will help tell us whether our "I wonder" statements are providing too much of a gentle nudge towards a topic or solution. Like a reliable and comfortable sweater that gets cozier the more you wear it, our active listening skills continue to strengthen the more we use them—helping us become even more effective attorneys _and_ counselors.